Tell Me Another

Tell Me Another

Storytelling and reading aloud at home, at school and in the community

Bob Barton

Pembroke Publishers Limited

Heinemann Educational Books Inc.

Copyright © 1986   Pembroke Publishers Limited
528 Hood Road
Markham, Ontario L3R 3K9

Library of Congress Cataloging-in-Publication Data

Barton, Bob.
   Tell me another.

Includes bibliographies and index.
1. Storytelling.   2. Oral reading.   I. Title.
LB1042.B37 1986   649'.58   86-18406
ISBN 0-435-08231-0 (Heinemann)

Typesetting: Jay Tee Graphics Limited

Manufactured in Canada by Webcom Limited
0 9 8 7 6 5 4 3 2

Table of contents

Introduction

Many fine books now in print address the art of storytelling in great detail. For the most part, I find that these books tend to deal with the subject in a formal way. For the purposes of this book, storytelling will be discussed in a broad context, which includes reading aloud.

The person who reads aloud to others is a storyteller, for he or she is charged with the same responsibility: to create a memorable experience.

In recent years, interest in storytelling has grown. As a result, a greater awareness of the role of the story and the process of creating the story, is beginning to emerge. Educational researchers, such as Gordon Wells who has conducted studies of children's language-development, claim that reading-progress and language-fluency in the early school years are largely dependent on the extent to which children have been exposed to stories and storytelling at home. Children who come to school without this exposure lack familiarity with the symbolic functions of language. Such children, says Wells, if they are to meet the language-demands that school will place on them, must be immediately exposed to storytelling and books on a one-to-one ratio the moment they arrive at the school doorstep.

Many teachers are convinced of the benefits of reading aloud to children every day, but there are still classrooms where this is not a priority. Sadly, as children get older, the chances of being read to diminish significantly, both at school and at home.

If parents wish to help their children make books and reading a part of their lives, shared experiences with stories are essential. For parents of older children who can read for themselves, there is no better way to keep the desire to read alive than by continuing a daily habit of reading aloud or storytelling.

It is my hope that after reading this book more teachers and parents will be less hesitant to perform aloud both with and without a book in front of them.

The potential to tell a story is in everyone. Each of us tells stories of our own life-experiences convincingly every day. When we are telling the stories of our lives, we muster the deepest feelings and interesting details we can to grip our listeners. Those skills that we use in such a natural way are the very ones required to carry out the activities in this book.

If there is one central message, it is simply that a willingness to explore and experiment is one of the greatest assets you can bring to the task of storytelling or reading aloud.

Storytelling is a dynamic form of communication. It is highly personal and its value is greater than just entertainment.

Storytelling reinforces the child's own storytelling skills, that fundamental grammar of all thought and communication, which enables each human being to order his or her experiences so they can be transmitted to others.

"By telling ourselves what happened, to whom and why we not only discover ourselves and the world, but we change and create ourselves and the world too."[1]

Early in my teaching career I discovered that sharing stories out loud with my classes was an excellent way to establish a positive relationship with them. Throughout twenty-five years it has never failed. Today, although I am no longer a regular classroom teacher, I still tell stories in my work.

My job requires that I do considerable public speaking and I always include a story in my address. Usually I start with a story in order to present, in metaphor, the substance of my talk and also to slow me down and get my thinking going. Just as important, a story permits me to establish a relationship with a roomful of strangers.

When a story is told so much is happening. For one thing, the storyteller reveals much about him or herself as a person. Listeners sense this quickly. They appreciate the storyteller's desire to reach out and make contact with them. Stories are wonderful meeting places. As author Janet Lunn puts it, "The whole world is one great conversation, which is carried out through telling stories and it is this great conversation that holds us together."

Recently a note, dictated by a group of kindergarten children to their teacher, arrived thanking me for visiting and telling stories. Included in the letter was this line, "When you said the words that helped us think the pictures."

1 Aidan, Chambers, "The Child's Changing Story", *Signal* (Winter 1983).

Children continue to remind me that listening to stories is important because it gives them the opportunity to think in the story world.

I am convinced that scores of children find that the mechanical challenges of silent reading prevent them from living in and through the life of the story as it unfolds.

When they listen to a story, the mechanical difficulties of reading are put aside and the storyteller's pacing, intonation, gestures and expression support their efforts to "think the pictures". (It goes without saying that the quality of the story is terribly important. Poor stories do not create such opportunities for the imagination.)

Far from being passive, the listener is extremely busy participating in the recreation of that story; for a successful listener needs to be a storyteller too. And this becomes an important reason for presenting stories out loud to children; it helps them to comprehend the role they are expected to play in the story game. This role will be the same when they read for themselves. Author Katherine Paterson describes this role: "My aim is to engage young readers in the life of a story which came out of me but which is not mine, but ours. I don't just want a young reader's time or attention, I want his life. I want his senses, his imagination, his intellect, his emotions and all the experiences he has known breathing life into the words upon the page. It doesn't matter how high my aim or how polished my craft, I know that without the efforts of my reader, I have accomplished nothing. The answer to the old puzzle about the tree falling in the unpopulated wilderness is that it makes no noise. I have not written a book for children unless the book is brought to life by the child who reads it. It is a co-operative venture. My aim is to do my part so well that the young reader will delight to join me as co-author."[2]

When we read or tell a story our aim is identical to that described by Katherine Paterson: to invite our listeners to join us as co-tellers. Therein lies the art of storytelling.

> "......storyteller and audience somehow constitute a single being, as inseparable as two lovers. One goes nowhere without the other. Either storyteller and audience are borne up together......or else they are left earthbound together, stranded, waiting for the small miracle to happen."

> Melvin Maddocks, *Time* August 1981.

2 Katherine Paterson, "The Aim of the Writer Who Writes for Children," *Theory Into Practice* Vol XXI No. 4 (Autumn 1982).

CHAPTER ONE
Little Sagas — Such as These

"An old woman is telling a story. She says it happened long ago, and she has had a cold ever since. Her nose runs on cold days, so there is a drop on the end of it now. She leaves it there."

from *Salt River Times*
William Mayne[3]

For many years, people have approached me following a storytelling session and confessed that although they enjoy listening to stories, they doubt they could actually get up in front of a group and tell one. There have been those who have admitted that they lack sufficient courage to read aloud. I have also met many people who are interested and enthusiastic about sharing stories out loud, but who aren't certain how to go about it. It is these experiences which have prompted me to offer some practical advice and suggestions for ways to get started.

We are all natural storytellers. Everything that happens to us in our lives is filed at the back of our minds in containers called stories.

Can you imagine a society where stories are not told:

"Who is your chronicler? Let me talk to her . . . . . to him."
At the blank looks Daughter-of-She-Who-Came-After
stamped her foot. "Who is the one who makes the songs of
your tribe's history and teaches the rest? Who remembers who

---

3 William Mayne, *Salt River Times*, Greenwillow.

was born in which moon of what year . . . . . who can tell the weather and what the harvest was like . . . . . Do not pretend to be stupid. You must tell me."

Benjamin shook his head. "We have no chronicler. The births and deaths are written in the Leut record, which the Preacher keeps. But we have no songs."

"Our only songs are the ones whereby we praise God," the Preacher snapped. "All else is vanity."

Daughter-of-She-Who-Came-After stared. "How can you be a tribe if you have no memory of who you are, or who your fathers and mothers were back to the beginning? If you cannot remember who it was who killed the great bear in the winter of little snow? If you cannot tell ahead in which years it will rain all through the summer because it has always done so in that kind of year? You are a people at the mercy of the moment if you do not reverence the past.

from *Beyond The Dark River*
Monica Hughes[4]

To be "at the mercy of the moment" is a terribly lonely prospect. What a strange world it would be without stories!

Everyone knows stories. They may be ones we heard as children, they may be ones we tell about our lives, but we all have them.

A few years ago, P.L. Travers, author of *Mary Poppins* (Harcourt), wrote a newspaper article entitled "Adventures Into Childhood." In the article, Travers told a story about three brothers who were new to her neighborhood. It seems that the boys tried to stink-bomb her mailbox and were caught in the act. In conversation afterwards with their father, Travers said of the boys, "It's just that they don't know where they are. They're lonely. They have no sense of place." She urged the father to spend more time with his sons and to help them develop a sense of place or *locality*. Make up stories about local shopkeepers, a hole in the road, works of public art, she pleaded. "This way you build your personal world like a bird building a nest. A straw here, a memory there —" For Travers, the possibilities for creating and telling stories were infinite.

---

4 Monica Hughes, *Beyond the Dark River*, Atheneum.

This advice remains fixed in my memory. What a wonderful, practical idea for parents and teachers — get involved with your children through your own stories!

When I meet people interested in learning about storytelling, I often have them start with their own stories. Many of these are *home stories*, which normally don't have much appeal beyond the intimacy of the family, but do trigger remembrances in others and get a wealth of stories flowing.

Nicholas Tucker, who teaches developmental psychology at the University of Sussex, observes that these home stories serve many important functions. He agrees with P.L. Travers that such stories are terribly important for developing a strong sense of home, of neighborhood and of community. He also points out that the child is often the center of these tales. He or she is the hero or heroine and the immediacy of such stories connects powerfully with the child and may even assist the child to overcome fears and anxieties.

In our home, my wife engaged in this kind of storytelling with our children. They were not the center of amazing fantasies, but they were the feature characters of simple home adventures. Mostly these stories were about a time in their lives that they were too young to remember. To this day, my now grownup children still request those stories: "Tell me about the time when I was three years old and drove our neighbor's car down Chedoke Avenue while she was carrying groceries into the house."

Traditional lore is also part of home stories. Much of it survives in the form of chants and rhymes, songs, superstitions and maxims. I seldom meet a person who can't remember a fragment of this lore.

Recently I was delighted to find a book entitled *Rhymes Around the Day*[5] because it highlights the potential of traditional rhymes as a beginning point for storytelling. The book revolves around the activities of three children and their parents from sunrise to sunset. Each of the day's activities has an accompanying rhyme. The book shows that simple stories can be enjoyed during the many important times when children and parents are together: bedtime, bake time, bath time, tooth brushing time.

The impact of this kind of home story is also beautifully documented in Alice Kane's *Songs and Sayings of an Ulster Childhood* where "everything was an occasion for a verse a song or a wild cry of delight or protest".

5 Omerod/Thompson, *Rhymes Around the Day*, Kestrel.

All of the rhymes, songs, sayings and chants in the book are set within a context of family and community, thus heightening the impact of the material.

> *My first real memories are of Mother, whom we called Mummy, mostly shadowy ones and mostly having to do with getting bathed or dressed. A very clear picture is the one of being lifted out of a bath, wrapped in a large towel which covered me from head to foot and being rubbed vigorously to a cry of 'Where's the baby? Where's the baby? Oh, there she is!'*
> *After the towelling my feet were dried carefully to the rhyme:*
> *This little piggy went to market*
> *This little piggy stayed at home*
> *This little piggy had bread and butter*
> *But this little piggy had none*
> *And this little piggy cried 'Wee wee wee'*
> *All the way home.*[6]

As a young teacher with little time to learn a folk or a fairy tale after lesson preparation, nursery rhymes became a mainstay of my storytelling repertoire.

At first I looked for pieces rich in sound and with strong, driving rhythms that the children and I could chant together.

> *One-ery, two-ery, ziccary, zan;*
> *Hollow bone, crackabone ninery ten:*
> *Spittery spot, it must be done;*
> *Twiddleum, twaddleum Twenty one.*

But the more I searched the nursery rhyme collections, the more fascinated I became with their forceful, direct language. . . .

> *Cross-patch,*
> *Draw the latch*
> *Sit by the fire and spin;*
> *Take a cup*
> *And drink it up,*
> *Then call your neighbors in.*

6 Alice Kane, *Songs and Sayings of an Ulster Childhood*, McClelland and Stewart.

Where have you been today, Billy, my son?
Where have you been today my only man?
I've been a wooing, mother, make my bed soon,
For I'm sick at heart, and fain would lay down.

What have you ate today, Billy my son?
What have you ate today, my only man?
I've ate eel-pie, mother, make my bed soon,
For I'm sick at heart, and shall die before noon.

In these powerful nursery rhymes, there lurked echoes of legends, myths, hero tales and ballads. For example, "Where have you been today, Billy my son?" echoes the ballad *Lord Randal* in eight lines.

I began to pay close attention to these stories and to search for connections. Far from being just fun and nonsense, these rhymes turned out to have intricate family trees and relatives all over the world.

On Saturday night I lost my wife
And where do you think I found her?
Up in the moon, singing a tune
With all the stars around her.

How strange, this woman's exit into space! Had she gone willingly? What did her singing have to do with the incident? Did anyone try to go after her? How did she adapt to a new environment? Was she able to return? What would she miss from her earthly home?

My quest for answers to these questions yielded myths and folktales too numerous to catalog completely: "The Star Maiden"[7], "The Star Brides" (p. 128 chapter six), "Why the Man in the Moon Is Happy"[8] and the remarkable Gabon tale from West Africa in Penelope Farmer's, *Beginnings* (Atheneum).

The familiar "Ring a ring o' roses, a pocket full of posies" sat cheek-by-jowl with the bizarre:

7 Virginia Haviland, *North American Legends*, Philomel.

8 Ronald Melzack, *Why the Man in the Moon Is Happy*, McClelland and Stewart.

There was an old woman, her name it was Peg;
Her head was of wood and she wore a cork leg.
The neighbors all pitched her into the water,
Her leg was drowned first, and her head followed after.

There were well-developed sagas such as this one that Maurice Sendak used for *Hector Protector* and *As I Went Over The Water* (Harper and Row).

Hector Protector was dressed all in green
Hector Protector was sent to the queen.
The queen did not like him; no more did the king.
So Hector Protector was sent home again.

tall tales about a Derby Ram whose wool:

Reached up into the sky
The eagles build their nests there
For I heard the young ones cry.

and short stories like the one about the old woman whose pig refused to jump over the stile.

Structure in the nursery rhyme literature also caught my interest.

Old woman, old woman
Shall we go a' shearing?

Speak a little louder, sir,
I'm very thick of hearing.

Old woman, old woman
Wilt thee go a'gleanin?

Speak a little louder, sir,
I cannot tell the meanin.

Old woman, old woman,
Wilt thee go a'walkin?

Speak a little louder, sir,
Or what's the use of 'talkin'.

Old woman, old woman,
Shall I come and kiss thee?

I think I hear some better, sir,
The Lord in Heaven bless ye.

The question and answer format of selections such as "Old woman, old woman" was everywhere — folk songs, poetry, short stories, playground lore:

Old buzzard old buzzard
What are you doing?
Picking up sticks.
What are you doing that for?
To build a fire.
Why do you need a fire?
To roast a chick.
Where will you get it?
Out of your flock!

It was a structure my students could quickly adapt to their own writing, so *question and answer* as a story-container was explored.
Such stories also created opportunities for the listeners to take a role, responding to the questions once the story was familiar.

What's in there?
Gold and money.
Where's my share?
The mousie's run away with it.
Where's the mousie?
In her housie.
Where's the housie?
In the woods.
Where's the woods?
The fire burnt it.
Where's the fire?
The water quenched it.
Where's the water?
The brown bull drank it.
Where's the brown bull?
Back o' Burnie's Hill.

Where's Burnie's Hill?
All clad in snow.
Where's the snow?
The sun melted it.
Where's the sun?
High, high in the sky.

Infinity stories became a favorite activity. We made a game of it; I would tell an infinity story and as soon as the children figured out how the story was working they would chime in. The fun was to be first one to chime in and to have guessed correctly.

It was a dark and stormy night
And I was standing on the deck
And the captain said to me,
"Tell me a story my boy!"
So I began.
It was a dark and stormy night, etc.

The boy octopus said to the girl octopus
"Want to walk along the beach
hand in hand, hand in hand, hand in hand, etc.

But the favorite was always:

Pete and Repete sat on a fence
Pete fell off
Who was left?
Repete!
Pete and Repete sat on a fence
. . . . and so on

All of this was so close to the children's own body of oral literature that they were soon swapping stories with me.

What's green and comes out at night?
(A vampickle.)

I had to be re-educated by my students. Indeed, there were few of them who knew nursery rhymes and many who had only recently heard the "three threes" — "Three Bears," "Three Pigs" and "Three

Billy Goats Gruff," but they had their own stories that they told with incredible skill and took great pride in teaching me. If only I had had the foresight then to record what they recited. Years later when I read Iona and Peter Opie's *The Lore and Language of School Children* (Oxford), I realized what opportunities I had missed.

Infinity stories led to cumulative stories. ("This is the house that Jack Built") and chronological stories ("Solomon Gundy") and rhyme rhythm patterns ("I had a cat and the cat pleased me, I fed my cat by yonder tree; Cat goes fiddle-i-fee"). All of these were story patterns the children could borrow for their own stories and they did.

In the process of sharing these stories the children and I were growing in our expressiveness and our willingness to experiment with our voices. Before long we were playing with words and looking for new roles; new ways to release print from the pages of our source material.

With little stories such as

There are men in the village of Erith
Whom nobody seeth or heareth
And there looms on the marge of the river a barge
That nobody roweth or steereth.

We tried to imagine who the storyteller might be and his or her purpose for telling the story.

Soon the story was told again and again by the voices of those newly returned from the dead; by the sirens who haunted the river; by weeping women who awaited the return of their menfolk from battle; by scolding grannies who had invented the story as a ploy to keep visiting grandchildren away from the water's edge.

As I look back, I realize how effortlessly I eased into storytelling. At the same time, the oral tradition with its built-in tricks (rhyme, rhythm, repetition) was doing for me what it had done for all human beings since the dawn of storytelling — helping me to remember.

CHAPTER TWO
Don't Tell Us Any of Those "Once Upon a Time Stories"

We all tell stories, but ours are mostly about what's happened to us or what we think has happened to us. Stanley's are weird. He tells stories about how when the sun goes down at night it turns into a golden fish and swims about and that's why you must never go into the water at night or you might make it angry and it won't come up again in the morning. He tells stories about how the stars sing and how you can catch the wind if you run fast enough and he says there are animals who live in the clouds. Look, he says you can see the shapes of them. Freda says, "That's not true, Stanley. You're only making that up, aren't you?"

from *The Voyage of QV 66*
Penelope Lively[9]

The unruly band of nine-year-olds burst into the library, galumphed across the room and threw themselves down on the carpet at my feet.

"Watcha gonna do with us mister?" they asked.

"I've come to tell you a story." I replied.

There was an immediate wrinkling of noses and screwing up of faces, accompanied by a chorus of groans.

"Don't you like stories?" I asked.

"Don't tell us any of those 'Once Upon A Time Stories!'" a girl close to my knees ordered.

"What's a 'Once Upon A Time Story'?" I asked innocently.

"You know," they all snorted, "those fairy stories."

"What would you like instead?" I asked.

9 Penelope Lively, *The Voyage of QV 66*, Piccolo.

"We want action!" they demanded.

I immediately launched into a Serbian fairytale, carefully omitting the "Once Upon a Time" opening. At the conclusion of the story, there was much nodding of heads and all round agreement that the story had been pretty good.

"Do you know," said the outspoken young lady beside my knees, "that's just like the soaps on TV!"

She was certainly close, for that fairytale was indeed the stuff of melodrama. It was more however. It was also a powerful imaginative experience and those difficult-to-reach children had been swept along by it.

But the children made an important point; they wanted a story with action. When choosing a story to share aloud this is something that must be kept in mind.

How to Select a Story:

Giving advice about story selection is tricky. We aren't all interested in the same stories. Stories are a very personal matter.

You will find yourself sifting through literally dozens of stories in order to find one that appeals to you. Don't be discouraged. Just when you think you'll never find a story you like, up it pops. I spend hours and hours poring through anthologies and most of what I have learned and continue to learn is by trial and error. It is in actually telling the story that so much about the story is discovered. Often I will tell a story a few times and then drop it. What I thought I liked about the story when I first found it, has not worked out. You have to really like a story to tell it well. Your confidence in a story goes a long way toward helping you put it across sincerely. The story should also have some quality that makes it worth sharing. What truths, images, discoveries, does it contain? How does it help us to understand humanity? In his *Read-Aloud Handbook* (Penguin) Jim Trelease says, "More than helping them to read better, more than exposing them to good writing, more than developing their imaginations, when we read aloud to children we are helping them to find themselves and to discover some meaning in the scheme of things."

For several summers, when I did a storytelling residency at the fabulous Artpark in Lewiston, New York, I was faced with an interesting selection problem. The majority of audiences that came to the storytelling theater were composed of adults, yet at any given moment the audience might contain preschoolers, adolescents, seniors and all categories in between. I soon learned that a good story was a good story for everyone; even young children can understand a good deal more when listening than they can when reading for themselves.

Working with varied audiences and paying attention to what worked and what didn't helped me to develop some guidelines for story selection. The following chart shows what a storyteller might keep in mind when matching stories and audiences.

Audience	Characteristics of Stories	Examples
A	— wide age range (toddlers to seniors) — new to storytelling sessions — often restless, noisy, difficult to hold	— short sharp pieces to open and close — slow, quiet material once listening has become focused — audience participation	— folktales; examples: "The Name" in *The Magic Orange Tree* Diane Wolkstein *The Crane Wife* Katherine Paterson
B	— controled, such as a school visit, luncheon entertainment — homogeneous group, numbers about average class size — some did not choose to attend	— a strong dramatic opening story — subtleties of humor (not off the top) — material should not seem frivolous or babyish	— authored tales, modern retellings of vintage works; examples: *Come Again in the Spring* Richard Kennedy
C	— festival, theater or classroom where storytelling is a regular occurance — listeners catch every nuance of a story and respond openly and enthusiastically — know stories well	— quality of listening permits subtlety — richly-textured well constructed pieces — length of story no problem	— retellings of traditional material and authored tales — complex traditional and modern material; examples: *The Dancing Tigers* Russell Hoban *The Wild Swans* Hans Christian Andersen

As indicated earlier, you have to love the story you are going to tell and if you tell it well, you should be able to tell it to anyone. Experience, however, has taught me that paying close attention to the group with whom I am sharing stories can help to make the experience easier on me and more enjoyable for the listeners.

A fast-paced and amusing story can work very well with a large and widely varied audience. An example would be Malcolm Carrick's retelling of an African folktale, *I Can Squash Elephants.*

The story is a cacaphony of threats and counter-threats. When Hare arrives at his cave he spies strange footprints leading into it and plaintively cries, "Who's there! Who's in Hare's house?" The cheeky caterpillar inside calls out "It's me!" The cave's echo creates a thundering retort that sends Hare scampering into the jungle for help. Some of the jungle's most powerful lords and ladies prance up to the mouth of the cave and attempt to dislodge the intruder, only to find themselves fleeing "the great dark beast".

We know who is in the cave; the *animals* do not. We can sit back and watch the "jungle heavies" strut their stuff, glorifying in their own self-importance; then derive great satisfaction as each in turn is brought down. The element of surprise makes this story successful. It is a quality I look for in each and every story I select.

If I had to choose a story that has *everything* my nod would go to "Owl" a wonderful Haitian folktale in Diane Wolkstein's, *The Magic Orange Tree.*

From its arresting opening line, "Owl thought he was ugly," through to an ending which moves you from shock to laughter to hushed stillness; the story grips you and never lets go. It is a tale of extreme differences and how those differences can mar the life of an individual. Owl's incredible lack of self-confidence is made even more painful by the presence of his cock-sure cousin, Rooster.

The song and dance sequences in the story provide a glorious opportunity for audience involvement and bring some comic relief to a very intense situation.

The Crane Wife (Morrow),   retold by Sumiko Yagawa, translated by Katherine Paterson, is a hauntingly beautiful Japanese folktale, which casts an eerie suspenseful mood.

A poor peasant marries a mysterious stranger and gains access to a peace and happiness the likes of which he has never known. He loses it because of his inability to pay attention to the important advice offered to him. Spare in style, every word carries weight as the story unfolds rapidly and flows steadily to its shocking conclusion. It is a minor masterpiece and never fails to capture the listener.

All these folktales work extremely well with less experienced story-goers. As strenuous as working with a "drop-in" audience can be, I often feel more at ease in situations where people can walk out if they aren't interested, than with a captive audience, which has been herded willy-nilly to listen to the storyteller. Groups of young adolescents can present quite a challenge in such situations. Initially they are reluctant to show any signs of interest or responsiveness. Some have never heard a story told aloud and think the whole thing somewhat beneath them. For these groups, I choose highly suspenseful stories and hook the listener very quickly.

Undoubtedly, one of the best examples is Richard Kennedy's *Come Again in the Spring*. In this miniature drama, a feisty old man named Hark finds himself caught up in a life and death battle of wits with the Grim Reaper. The plot is fast-paced and episodic and the outcome is in doubt right up to the last few lines. It is a cliffhanger and a very satisfying experience. I doubt anyone would ever tire of telling this story.

Whenever storytelling is described, the word *spell* is often used. A story that really does cast a spell is the wonderful modern fairy-tale, *The Spider's Palace* by Richard Hughes. Initially, I thought this a good story for younger children, but I have been pleasantly surprised to discover that teenagers and adults are even more intrigued by it.

The story is set in a tangly, snake-infested forest with a girl poised "on the edge of the twigs where even the snakes were too terrified to come after her", ready for her ascent into the clouds on the back of a spider. Magic is everywhere. Anything can happen and it does. The subject-matter is compelling, the situation is serious and the matter-of-fact tone of the language holds everyone in thrall. Truly it is an extraordinary story.

One ten-year-old girl had this comment to make about it, "I am crazy to know what happened to the girl after she saw the spider turn into a man. Will they live happily ever after? I like those stories a lot, they make you have to imagine what would happen next."

Need I say more?

From a collection of four stories by Russell Hoban *La Corona and the Tin Frog* (Jonathan Cape/Merrimack, dist.) works well out loud. It is a tiny story, exacting in detail, yet large in possibilities. It is about a love affair between a wind-up frog and the beautiful lady found on the label inside the lid of a cigar box. The romance takes place entirely inside the cigar box with a supporting cast that includes a magnifying glass, a seashell and a yellow, cloth measuring tape. Hoban creates a fascinating world inside that cigar box. Even the most cynical teenagers have hung keenly to every word.

My third audience-category is a storyteller's dream. They listen so intensely that each word-sound seems larger than ever and you are buoyed up and whisked along. These folks have come to listen, they know stories and they mean business. You can indulge yourself in long, complicated stories, such as Hans Christian Andersen's *The Wild Swans*. This is not to say you can't tell this story to the other audiences. You can, but working between the story and the listener can be exhausting. With an experienced audience, I can settle into the story, take my time and make every moment count. No abbreviating, no rushing will be necessary.

Regardless of audience, all of the stories mentioned have a small number of characters and lots of action, rather than lengthy description.

Stories live through their characters. When Old Hark, Owl, La Corona and the Crane Wife enter our lives, they are not forgotten quickly. That is why a keen awareness of character is extremely important in choosing stories.

Listening to others read and tell stories is also useful in story selection. We don't all like the same stories, so it is important to find out what stories appeal to others and why. Many-a-time I have passed over a story only to hear someone else tell it and realize, through another's viewpoint, aspects of the story I had never considered. For this reason, I have never been too concerned if the story I tell is one with which the listeners are familiar.

The storyteller is an interpreter who should help the listener experience new meanings and new insights from the story. When you tell a story, you are the go-between who has carefully worked with the story and who imparts nuances and innuendoes with your voice, gestures and facial expressions. Each time a story is told, it is born again for the listeners and for the storyteller.

Finding Stories:

There are thousands of stories from which to make your choices, but you will not go wrong with folktales. Continuous shaping and re-shaping through countless tellings by generation after generation have resulted in a wonderful economy of words and beauty of structure.

Molly Bang's retelling of the Indian folktale, *The Old Woman and the Rice Thief* is a good example.

In this rollicking romp, an old woman who has been robbed repeatedly of her "cold boiled rice and her warm puffed rice" decides to take matters into her own hands and complain to the local Rajah.

Along the road to the Rajah's palace she meets a scorpion fish, a wood apple, a cow pat, a razor blade and a crocodile, who all offer to give assistance. The old woman turns them down at first, but eventually is forced to relent and the results are explosive.

Since the structure of this tale is both cumulative and repetitive, even the youngest listener can figure out how the story is working and begin to predict what will happen next. At the same time, there is an opportunity for the audience to participate in the story. For example, "I'll be the old woman; you be the razor blade. What do you say?" It is this opportunity to join in that makes this story so much fun for both the storyteller and the listeners. Stories such as this one are known as formula tales. Generally their structure is quite simple, yet they contain some of the best qualities not only of folktales, but of storytelling; they are action-packed and the repetition and refrains propel them along briskly.

These story patterns offer children the opportunity to play with language and story structure and help them to see the possibilities language offers to them. Of course such stories are ideal for reading aloud as well as telling, but it seems to me a shame to read them because they are so easily learned.

In addition to the cumulative pattern, here are a few more examples of formula tales:

Recurring Pattern:

You may be familiar with the story "In a dark, dark woods there was a dark, dark house. In the dark, dark house there was a dark, dark room" and so on. The same words recur again and again; each time adding a new detail to advance the story. *The Gold in the Chimley* has a very similar structure; incidents and words are repeated again and again. *The Gold in the Chimley* story is also a little *cante tale*, meaning that parts of it can be sung. Invent your own tune for the witch's recurring question:

> *Cowel o mine, cowel o mine,*
> *Have you ever seen a maid o mine.*
> *With a wig and a wag and a long leather bag,*
> *Who stold all the money I ever had?*

and invite your listeners to join you in the telling.

Once upon a time there was two girls. They were sisters, and one went to a witch's house to get a place to stay. Well, the witch said, "All right, you can stay." Said, "I'm goin to the store and don't you look up the chimley while I'm gone."

While she was gone she looked up the chimley. There hung a bag of gold. She got this gold and started, and come to a cow. The cow says, "Please milk me, little girl, I hain't been milked in several long years."

She says, "I hain't got time."

She went to a sheep and the sheep said, "Please shear me, little girl, I hain't been sheared in several long years."

She says, "I hain't got time."

She went on to a horse, and the horse said, "Please ride me, little girl, I hain't been rode in several long years."

She said, "I hain't got time."

She went on and come to a mill. The mill said, "Please turn me, little girl, I hain't been turned in several long years."

The little girl said, "I hain't got time." She went over and laid down behind the door and went to sleep.

Well, the old witch come back, and her gold was gone. She started out and come to the cow and said,

Cowel o mine, cowel o mine,
Have you ever seen a maid o mine.
With a wig and a wag and a long leather bag,
Who stold all the money I ever had?

She said, "Yeau, she just passed."
Went on to the sheep, said,

Sheep o mine, sheep o mine,
Have you ever seen a maid o mine,
With a wig and a wag and a long leather bag,
Who stold all the money I ever had?

She said, "Yeau, she just passed."
She went on to the horse and said,

Horse o mine, horse o mine,
Have you ever seen a maid o mine,
With a wig and a wag and a long leather bag,
Who stold all the money I ever had?

The horse said, "Yeau, she just passed."
She went on to the mill and said,

Mill o mine, mill o mine,
Have you ever seen a maid o mine,
With a wig and a wag and a long leather bag,
Who stold all the money I ever had?

It said, "She's layin over there behind the door."
She went over there and turned her into a stone. She got
her gold and went on back home.

Well, the next girl come along and said, "Can I get to stay
here?"

She said, "Yeau, but I'm going to the store," and said, "don't
look up the chimley while I'm gone."

When she got gone she looked up the chimley. There hung
this bag of gold. She got it and started. Come to this cow,
and the cow said, "Please milk me, little girl, I hain't been
milked in several long years."

She milked the cow. Went on to the sheep. The sheep said,
"Please shear me, little girl. I hain't been sheared in several
long years."

She sheared the sheep. Went on to the horse. The horse
said, "Please ride me, little girl. I hain't been rode in several
long years."

So she rode the horse. Come to the mill. The mill says,
"Please turn me, little girl. I hain't been turned in several long
years."

She turned the mill.

Well, the old witch come back, and her gold was gone. She
started. She come to the cow and said,

Cowel o mine, cowel o mine,
Have you ever seen a maid o mine,
With a wig and a wag and a long leather bag,
Who stold all the money I ever had?

She said, "No."
She went to the sheep —

Sheep o mine, sheep o mine,
Have you ever seen a maid o mine,
With a wig and a wag and a long leather bag,
Who stold all the money I ever had?

Said, "No, I hain't never seen her."
Went on to the horse and said,

Horse o mine, horse o mine,
Have you ever seen a maid o mine,
With a wig and a wag and a long leather bag,
Who stold all the money I ever had?

Said, "No, I hain't never seen her."
She went on to the mill and said,

Mill o mine, mill o mine,
Have you ever seen a maid o mine,
With a wig and a wag and a long leather bag,
Who stold all the money I ever had?

It said, "Get up in my hopper, I can't hear good."
She got up in the hopper and said,

MILL O MINE, MILL O MINE,
HAVE YOU EVER SEEN A MAID O MINE,
WITH A WIG AND A WAG AND A LONG LEATHER BAG,
WHO STOLD ALL THE MONEY I EVER HAD?

The mill started grinding and ground her up.

The little girl she got up, turned the stone back into her sister and they lived happily ever after.

Sequential Pattern:

If you look back to the nursery rhyme *Burnie's Hill* (page 16) in chapter one you will notice that it is a sequential pattern. Sometimes stories such as these are called *swapping tales* in the way the ideas are linked. I often think of them as *windshield-wiper tales* swinging back and forth between question and answer (*Burnie's Hill*), alternating scenes (*King Nimrod's Tower*, Chapter Three) or in before and after sequences (*The Travels of a Fox*).

A fox digging behind a stump found a bumblebee. The fox put the bumblebee in his bag, and traveled.

The first house he came to he went in, and said to the mistress of the house, "Can I leave my bag here while I go to Squintum's?"

"Yes," said the woman.

"Then be careful not to open the bag," said the fox.

But as soon as the fox was out of sight the woman just took a little peep into the bag, and out flew the bumblebee, and the rooster caught him and ate him all up.

After a while the fox came back. He took up his bag, and he saw that his bumblebee was gone, and he said to the woman, "Where is my bumblebee?"

And the woman said, "I just untied the string, and the bumblebee flew out, and the rooster ate him up."

"Very well," said the fox; "I must have the rooster, then."

So he caught the rooster and put him in his bag, and traveled.

And the next house he came to he went in, and said to the mistress of the house, "Can I leave my bag here while I go to Squintum's?"

"Yes," said the woman.

"Then be careful not to open the bag," said the fox.

But as soon as the fox was out of sight the woman just took a little peek into the bag, and the rooster flew out, and the pig caught him and ate him all up.

After a while the fox came back. He took up his bag, and he saw that his rooster was gone, and he said to the woman, "Where is my rooster?"

And the woman said, "I just untied the string, and the rooster flew out and the pig ate him up."

"Very well," said the fox; "I must have the pig, then."

So he caught the pig and put him in his bag, and traveled.

And the next house he came to he went in, and said to the mistress of the house, "Can I leave my bag here while I go to Squintum's?"

"Yes," said the woman.

"Then be careful not to open the bag," said the fox.

But as soon as the fox was out of sight the woman just took a little peep into the bag, and the pig jumped out, and the ox gored him.

After a while the fox came back. He took up his bag, and he saw that his pig was gone, and he said to the woman, "Where is my pig?"

And the woman said, "I just untied the string, and the pig jumped out, and the ox gored him."

"Very well," said the fox; "I must have the ox, then."

So he caught the ox and put him in his bag, and traveled.

And the next house he came to he went in, and said to the mistress of the house, "Can I leave my bag here while I go to Squintum's?"

"Yes," said the woman.

"Then be careful not to open the bag," said the fox.

But as soon as the fox was out of sight the woman just took a little peep, and the ox got out, and the woman's little boy broke off his horns and killed him.

After a while the fox came back. He took up his bag, and he saw that his ox was gone, and he said to the woman, "Where is my ox?"

And the woman said, "I just untied the string, and the ox got out, and my little boy broke off his horns and killed him."

"Very well," said the fox; "I must have the little boy, then."

So he caught the little boy and put him in his bag, and traveled.

And the next house he came to he went in, and said to the

mistress of the house, "Can I leave my bag here while I go to Squintum's?"

"Yes," said the woman.

"Then be careful not to open the bag," said the fox.

The woman was making cake, and her children were around her teasing for it.

"Oh, ma, give me a piece!" said one, and "Oh, ma, give me a piece!" said the others.

And the smell of the cake came to the little boy weeping and crying in the bag, and he heard the children beg for the cake, and he said, "Oh, mammy, give me a piece!"

Then the woman opened the bag and took the little boy out, and she put the house-dog in the bag in the little boy's place. And the little boy stopped crying and joined the other children.

After a while the fox came back. He took up his bag, and he saw that it was tied fast, and he put it on his back, and traveled deep into the woods. Then he sat down and untied the bag, and if the little boy had been in the bag things would have gone badly with him.

But the little boy was safe at the woman's house, and when the fox untied the bag the house-dog jumped out and caught the fox and killed him.

Just for fun, decide whether the next tale is cumulative, sequential or recurring. This tale will probably remind you of a familiar version from *Italian Folktales* (Harcourt) collected by Italo Calvino.

Don't be surprised if you have difficulty deciding, for all of these pattern stories contain varieties of combinations.

CRYSTAL ROOSTER

There was once a rooster that went strutting about the world. He found a letter lying in the road, picked it up with his beak, and read:

Crystal Rooster, Crystal Hen, Countess Goose, Abbess Duck, Goldfinch Birdie: Let's be off to Tom Thumb's wedding.

The rooster set out in that direction, and shortly met the hen.

"Where are you going, brother rooster?"
"I'm going to Tom Thumb's wedding?"
"May I come, too?"
"If you're mentioned in the letter."
He unfolded the letter again and read: Crystal Rooster, Crystal Hen . . . "Here you are, here you are, so let's be on our way."
They continued onward together. Before long they met the goose.
"Oh, sister hen and brother rooster! Where are you going?"
"We are going to Tom Thumb's wedding?"
"May I come, too?"
"If you're mentioned in the letter."
The rooster unfolded the letter again and read: Crystal Rooster, Crystal Hen, Countess Goose . . . "Here you are, so let's be on our way!"
The three of them walked and walked and soon met the duck.
"Where are you going, sister goose, sister hen, and brother rooster?"
"We are going to Tom Thumb's wedding?"
"May I come, too?"
"Yes, indeed, if you are mentioned here." He read: Crystal Rooster, Crystal Hen, Countess Goose, Abbess Duck . . . "You're here all right, so join us!"
Before long they met the goldfinch birdie.
"Where are you going, sister duck, sister goose, sister hen, and brother rooster?"
"We are going to Tom Thumb's wedding."
"May I come, too?"
"Yes, indeed, if you're mentioned here!"
He unfolded the letter again: Crystal Rooster, Crystal Hen, Countess Goose, Abbess Duck, Goldfinch Birdie . . . "You are here too."
So all five of them walked on together.
Lo and behold, they met the wolf, who also asked where they were going.
"We are going to Tom Thumb's wedding," replied the rooster.
"May I come, too?"
"Yes, if you're mentioned here!"

The rooster reread the letter, but it made no mention of the wolf.

"But I want to come!" said the wolf.

Out of fear they all replied, "All right, let's all go."

They'd not gone far when the wolf suddenly said, "I'm hungry."

The rooster replied, "I've nothing to offer you. . ."

"I'll just eat you, then!" He opened his mouth wide and swallowed the rooster whole.

Further on he again said, "I'm hungry."

The hen gave him the same answer as the rooster had, and the wolf gobbled her up too. And the goose and the duck went the same way.

Now there was just the wolf and the birdie. The wolf said, "Birdie, I'm hungry!"

"And what do you expect me to give you?"

"I'll just eat you. then!"

He opened his mouth wide . . . and the bird perched on his head. The wolf tried his best to catch him, but the bird flitted all around, hopped from branch to branch, then back to the wolf's head and on to his tail, driving him to distraction. When the wolf was completely exhausted, he spied a woman coming down the road with the reapers' lunch in a basket on her head. The bird called to the wolf, "If you spare my life, I'll see that you get a hearty meal of noodles and meat which that woman is bringing the reapers. As soon as she sees me, she'll want to catch me. I'll fly off and hop from branch to branch. She'll put her basket down and come after me. Then you can go and eat everything up."

That's just what happened. The woman came up, spied the beautiful little bird, and immediately reached out to catch him. He then flew off a little way, and she put down her basket and ran after him. So the wolf approached the basket and started eating.

"Help! Help!" screamed the woman. The reapers came running with scythes and sticks, pounced upon the wolf, and killed him. Out of his belly, safe and sound, hopped crystal rooster, crystal hen, countess goose, abbess duck, and together with goldfinch birdie they all went to Tom Thumb's wedding.

Quest:

The important aspect in the Quest pattern is the journey. Usually some major crisis sets the adventure in motion.

The Old Woman and the Rice Thief is also about quest and it is the actions of the thief that cause events to get under way.

Maggie Duff's retelling of the Indian folktale *Rum Pum Pum* (Macmillan) is another good example.

In additon to structural patterns, the oral tradition presents us with story conventions that aid the memory. Such conventions include the rule of three — three wishes, three attempts — youngest son, youngest daughter and so on.

Read *I'm Tipingee, She's Tippingee, We're Tipingee, Too* and note the conventions.

"I'M TIPINGEE, SHE'S TIPINGEE, WE'RE TIPINGEE, TOO"

There was once a girl named Tipingee who lived with her stepmother. Her father was dead. The stepmother was selfish, and even though she lived in the girl's house she did not like to share what she earned with the girl.

One morning, the stepmother was cooking sweets to sell in the market. The fire under her pot went out. Tipingee was in school, so the stepmother had to go herself into the forest to find more firewood. She walked for a long time, but she did not find any wood. She continued walking. Then she came to a place where there was firewood everywhere. She gathered it into a bundle. But it was too heavy to lift up onto her head. Still, she did not want anyone else to have any of the firewood. So standing in the middle of the forest she cried out: "My friends, there is so much wood here and at home I have no wood. Where can I find a person who will help me carry the firewood?"

Suddenly an old man appeared. "I will help you to carry the firewood. But then what will you give me?"

"I have very little," the woman said, "but I will find something to give you when we get to my house."

The old man carried the firewood for the stepmother, and when they got to the house he said, "I have carried the firewood for you. Now what will you give me?"

"I will give you a servant girl. I will give you my stepdaughter, Tipingee."

Now Tipingee was in the house, and when she heard her name she ran to the door and listened.

"Tomorrow I will send my stepdaughter to the well at noon for water. She will be wearing a red dress, call her by her name, Tipingee, and she will come to you. Then you can take her."

"Very well," said the man, and he went away.

Tipingee ran to her friends. She ran to the houses of all the girls in her class and asked them to wear red dresses the next day.

At noon the next day the old man went to the well. He saw one little girl dressed in red. He saw a second little girl dressed in red. He saw a third girl in red.

"Which of you is Tipingee?" he asked.

The first little girl said: "I'm Tipingee."

The second little girl said: "She's Tipingee."

The third little girl said: "We're Tipingee, too."

"Which of you is Tipingee?" asked the old man.

Then the little girls began to clap and jump up and down and chant:

I'm Tipingee,
She's Tipingee,
We're Tipingee, too.
I'm Tipingee,
She's Tipingee,
We're Tipingee, too.

Rah! The old man went to the woman and said, "You tricked me. All the girls were dressed in red and each one said she was Tipingee."

"That is impossible," said the stepmother. "Tomorrow she will wear a black dress. Then you will find her. The one wearing a black dress will be Tipingee. Call her and take her."

But Tipingee heard what her stepmother said and ran and begged all her friends to wear black dresses the next day.

When the old man went to the well the next day, he saw one little girl dressed in black. He saw a second little girl dressed in black. He saw a third girl in black.

"Which of you is Tipingee?" he asked.

The first little girl said: "I'm Tipingee."

The second little girl said: "She's Tipingee."
The third little girl said: "We're Tipingee, too."
"Which of you is Tipingee?" asked the old man.
And the girls joined hands and skipped about and sang:
I'm Tipingee,
She's Tipingee,
We're Tippingee, too.
I'm Tipingee,
She's Tipingee,
We're Tipingee, too.
The man was getting angry. He went to the stepmother and
said, "You promised to pay me and you are only giving me
problems. You tell me Tipingee and everyone here is
Tipingee, Tipingee, Tipingee, Tipingee. If this happens a third
time, I will come and take you for my servant."
"My dear sir," said the stepmother, "tomorrow she will be in
red, completely in red, call her and take her."
And again Tipingee ran and told her friends to dress in red.
At noon the next day, the old man arrived at the well. He
saw one little girl dressed in red. He saw a second little girl
dressed in red. He saw a third girl in red.
"Which of you is Tipingee?" he asked.
"I'm Tipingee," said the first girl.
"She's Tipingee," said the second girl.
"We're Tipingee, too," said the third girl.
"WHICH OF YOU IS TIPINGEE?" the old man shouted.
But the girls just clapped and jumped up and down and
sang:
I'm Tipingee,
She's Tipingee,
We're Tipingee, too.
I'm Tipingee,
She's Tipingee,
We're Tipingee, too.
The old man knew he would never find Tipingee. He went
to the stepmother and took her away. When Tipingee
returned home, she was gone. So she lived in her own house
with all her father's belongings, and she was happy.

The following are formula tales you might want to try telling.

Cumulative

1. *Drummer Hoff*, Barbara and Ed Emberley, Prentice Hall.
2. *Euphonia and the Flood*, Mary Calhoun, Parents.
3. *The Fat Cat*, Jack Kent, Scholastic.
4. *The Terrible Tiger*, Jack Prelutsky, Collier Macmillan.
5. "This Is the House That Jack Built", *The Three Bears and Fifteen Other Stories*, Anne Rockwell, Crowell.

Sequential

1. *Over in the Meadow*, John Langstaff, Harcourt Brace Jovanovich.
2. *Little Pieces of the West Wind*, Christian Garrison, Bradbury.
3. *Goodnight Moon*, Margaret Wise Brown, Harper and Row.
4. *Brown Bear Brown Bear What Do You See?*, Bill Martin, Jr., Holt, Rinehart and Winston.
5. "Soap! Soap! Soap!", *Grandfather Tales*, Richard Chase, Houghton Mifflin.

Recurring

1. "The China Spaniel", *The Wonder Dog*, Richard Hughes, Greenwillow.
2. "Lambiken", *The Old Woman and Her Pig and Ten Other Stories*, Anne Rockwell, Crowell.
3. *Mrs. Fox's Wedding*, Sara and Stephen Corrin, Penguin.
4. "The Cat and the Mouse," *To Read and To Tell*, Norah Montgomerie, Bodley Head / Merrimack (dist.).
5. "The Golden Arm", *The Thing at the Foot of the Bed*, Maria Leach, Dell.

Quest

1. *Rum Pum Pum*, Maggie Duff, Macmillan.
2. *The Dream Eater*, Christian Garrison, Bradbury.
3. *The Little Hen and the Giant*, Maria Polushkin, Harper and Row.
4. *The Story of Jumping Mouse*, John Steptoe, Lothrop.
5. *Little Sister and the Month Brothers*, Beatrice de Regniers, Houghton Mifflin.

To assist you further, here are ten anthologies containing traditional material I have found valuable.

Folktales for Reading and Telling   Leila Berg   Hodder & Stoughton

This splendid collection of eighteen stories from nine countries is retold in a direct, lively style by Leila Berg. Many old favorites are included ("The Three Billy-Goats Gruff", "The Gingerbread Man", "Little Dog Turpie") as well as lesser known stories, which should prove just as popular ("Higgeldy-Piggeldy," "Topsy Turvey", "Rabbit and Elephant"). Included with the stories is a fine introduction to storytelling.

Of her selection she says: "There are no stories here of children abandoned by their parents, nor any acceptance of the superiority of boys or the habit of giving away girls as prizes. Folk tales have always changed, as the society that made them and received them back has changed. And every storyteller plays his part, writing or telling."

Fox Tricks   Aidan Chambers   Heinemann

The three Aesop's fables in this little book have been retold for young children to read for themselves. Nevertheless, Aidan Chambers' reworking of these fables is so well done that they make wonderful short pieces for storytelling.

Chambers has taken these eliptical fables and elaborated them so that the language flows along briskly and the overall effect is lively and interesting. For example:

> *"One day, Fox set out*
> *to find food for his family.*
> *'I must hurry,' he thought.*
> *His family was big and hungry.*
> *But Fox hurried too fast.*
> *He tripped into a well*
> *and could not get out.*
> *He struggled*
> *and splashed,*
> *but it was no good."*

A World of Fairy Tales   James Riordan   Hamlyn

Strictly speaking, the 25 tales in this anthology are drawn more from writers such as Hans Christian Andersen than from traditional folk sources. In this diverse and entertaining collection are "Jack and the Beanstalk", "Tom Thumb" and "Sleeping Beauty", but so too are "The Rainbow and the Bread Fruit Flower" (Australia), the "Aztec Sun" (Mexico) and "Children of the Wind" (Africa).

Of particular interest to me was "The Blue Baba of the Marsh", a tale from the Ural Mountains from the collection by the Russian ex-miner Pavel Bazhov who learned the folk history of the Urals while working in the copper mines and the gold fields.

In his notes, James Riordan says of the book, "In selecting tales for inclusion I have cast the net wide so as to take in different cultures for the benefit of our own modern multi-ethnic communities. And in an age when so many sexual stereotypes are being challenged, I have tried to strike a balance between stories featuring men and women as the heroes."

See also Riordan's *The Woman in the Moon and Other Tales of Forgotten Heroines* (Dial)

One Thousand and One Arabian Nights   Geraldine McCaughrean
Oxford

King Shahryar has married and killed a thousand brides but this doesn't deter the beautiful Shaharazad from begging her father, the Wazir, to permit her to marry the king.

Thus begins the account of 35 of the Nights (some in English for the first time) in this absolutely first-rate introduction to the famous Arabian Nights.

I can not say enough good things about this anthology. Humor, tragedy and suspense are deftly balanced in this outstanding recreation of a world famous collection and will appeal strongly to both children and adults. "The Everlasting Shoes", "The Tale of the Little Beggar", "The Lion's Revenge on Mankin" and "The Prince and the Large and Lonely Tortoise" are especially appealing.

A Book of Goblins   Alan Garner   Hamish Hamilton

For some reason, the title of this collection put me off and I deliberately passed over it for some time. When I did get around to reading it, I found myself faced with one of the most extraordinary collections of beings one could imagine.

Garner's adaptations and retellings of the folklore of many lands are brilliant. Among the collection are stories from Britain, Japan and the native peoples of North America. One such tale, "The Smoker", is wonderful to tell. So too is the Serbian fairytale "The Trade That No One Knows".

The Magic Horns Forbes Stuart Abelard Schuman

The eight tales that make up this collection have been gathered by the author from among the Bantus and the Hottentots of South Africa. The stories are simply told, but are often very moving and gently humorous.

The familiar "The Hare and the Tortoise" story is here, but in the earlier African version, not the Aesop version to which we are accustomed. Also included is "The Magic Tree" which is a long-time favorite of storytellers. All ages will enjoy this small, lively collection.

Coyote the Trickster Gail Robinson/Douglas Hill Chatto & Windus

Canadian writers Gail Robinson and Douglas Hill, who lived among the North American Indians for several years, have retold 12 stories of Coyote, the trickster of the Great Plains tribes, in this volume.

Among the native peoples of North America, there are many stories about a race of animal-gods who are supernatural, but also appear in the form of animals or humans.

There are many sides to the personality of the trickster and in these stories we are introduced to these several aspects. The final tale in the collection, "Coyote in the Land of the Dead," is especially beautiful and captivating.

The Magic Orange Tree Diane Wolkstein Knopf

This very special anthology of stories was collected by storyteller Diane Wolkstein during several visits to the island of Haiti during the 1970s.

Accompanying the stories is a splendid introduction which describes the background and the task faced by Diane in assembling the material. In addition, we are told before each story, the circumstances involving that story's telling in its natural setting.

Many of the 27 stories include a song or chorus which can be used to involve the listener. Musical scores for the songs are provided.

The appearance of these stories on records and in new anthologies is a testament to their power and impact. Stories such as "The Name" I have shared with pre-schoolers in the morning and senior English students in the afternoon with equally splendid results. Of course the popular tale of "Owl" is here as well as many other tales of laughter, mystery and suspense. There are wonderful surprises to be discovered in this collection.

North American Legends   Virginia Haviland   Philomel

An excellent overview of the myths, legends and folktales of North America has been provided by Virginia Haviland in this well-chosen collection.

By far the largest section of the book is devoted to the stories of the native peoples of North America. Among the stories you will find the "Star Maiden", referred to in the previous chapter and the very beautiful "Indian Cinderella" from Cyrus MacMillan's *Canadian Wonder Tales* (Bodley Head/Merrimack, dist.).

The three remaining sections contain splendid examples of tales from black Americans, European immigrants and tall tales of the "Paul Bunyan" and "Pecos Bill" variety.

Virginia Haviland has also included an excellent bibliography for readers eager to pursue further investigations of any of the sections.

Although the purpose of this survey of anthologies has been to assist you in finding folk material, there are two collections of contemporary stories which are highly recommended, *The Wonder Dog*, Richard Hughes, (Greenwillow) and *How The Whale Became and Other Stories*, Ted Hughes, (Penguin).

It could be argued that the stories of Richard Hughes were born of the oral tradition. In the foreword we learn that the stories written down were only a few of many told and that they survived because a listener told them back.

The Wonder Dog contains eighteen of the twenty stories first published in *The Spider's Palace* (1931) and ten of the thirteen stories from *Don't Blame Me* (1940). If the ability to make a story compelling and memorable is the work of a gifted storyteller then Hughes' work qualifies. I have told many of these modern fairytales including "The China Spaniel," "The Ants", "The Spider's Palace", "The Jungle School" to name a few; they have been a joy to learn and to tell. In Geoffrey Parker's review of this collection he said, "*The Wonder Dog* will stand in the open market as 180 pages of enthralling stories for children between the ages of five and ten. For this, we — and they — can Be Glad." I would add that a large number of teenagers and adults have been "Glad" also.

Once I was asked to tell a *trickster tale* as part of a storytelling festival. I turned immediately to poet Ted Hughes' *How the Whale Became*. There were several suitable stories in this collection, but I settled on "Why Owl Behaves as He Does". Among the traditional tricksters, Anansi, Raven and The Hodja, "Owl" stood up extremely well.

I have read and reread this collection several times and I keep discovering more material that I want to tell.

Although the stories may simply be explained away as modern *pourquoi tales* these sinewy stories, like favorite folktales, hold up to the light the selfishness, meanness, foolishness and vanity of humankind. You can't ask for better stories than "How the Bee Became" or the remarkable "How the Tortoise Became".

Tales of Magic and Enchantment   Kathleen Lines   Faber

Included in this very fine collection is a selection of fairytales and legends from different national traditions. Among the fairytales are some which will not be widely known. "The Feather of Finist the Falcon" (Russia) and "How the Raja's Son Won the Princess Lobam" (India) are examples.

There are 13 fairytales in all and then attention shifts to tales from the prose cycles and poems of medieval literature. Sources here include The Old Testament, Chaucer's *Canterbury Tales*, the Irish hero tales and the story of Beowulf. These latter extracts all serve as a good introduction to the hero tales and romantic legends which may be encountered later in a child's life.

There are two additional bodies of work which must be mentioned. Storyteller/anthologist Eileen Colwell and Ruth Manning-Sanders have contributed extensively to the gathering of stories. For the most part their choices are impeccable, but in each instance certain of their works have appealed to me more than others. In the case of Eileen Colwell I would strongly recommend her book *Humblepuppy* (The Bodley Head), a collection of traditional and contemporary stories. From among the prolific works of Ruth Manning-Sanders try *A Book of Magic Animals* (Methuen), folktales from around the world featuring creatures both real and imaginary.

OTHER GOOD SOURCES:

Canadian Fairy Tales,   Eva Martin and Laszlo Gal,   Groundwood.
Mouse Woman and the Mischief Makers,   Christie Harris,   Atheneum.
Stories for Children,   I.B. Singer,   Farrar, Straus & Giroux.
The War of the Birds and the Beasts,   Arthur Ransome,   Jonathan Cape/Merrimack (dist.).
Raven the Trickster,   Gail Robinson,   Atheneum.
The People Could Fly: American Black Folktales,   Virginia Hamilton, Knopf.
The Magic Fiddler and other Legends of French Canada,   Claude Aubry,   Clarke Irwin.
The Story Spirits,   Annabel Williams-Ellis,   Heinemann.
Seasons of Splendour: Tales, Myths and Legends of India,   Madhur Jaffrey,   Atheneum.
Tales of Wonder,   Jane Yolen,   Schocken.
Tales of South Asia (set of four books),   Beulah Candappa,   Ginn.
The Juniper Tree and Other Tales from Grimm, Lore Segal and Randall Jarrell (trans.), Farrar, Straus & Giroux.

Making the Story Your Own

"Always read a poem twice:
once for the words,
and then for the music of the words."

Eve Merriam[10]

Each of us must learn a story in our own way, but each story, too, will place its demands on us in terms of making it our own.

Some people learn best by listening. Repeated listenings to a tape recorded story serves them well. Some may prefer to write the story out in full or jot down a plot summary. Several slow readings over a period of time will suffice for others.

Regardless of how the story is approached, memorizing a plot is not storytelling. Stories are about people, ideas and feelings. To tell a story, involves remembering, identifying and interpreting. It is about exploring, experimenting and engaging in the life of the story. It might best be described as a building process.

When you set out to make a story yours, you must discover more about the story than you ever deemed possible. Extensive research yields one kind of learning, but that isn't what I am referring to. What I have in mind is the kind of imaginative exploration that takes you into every nook and cranny of the story. It's not unlike Eve Merriam's advice in the opening quotation. Among the foundation blocks to be considered are story structure, character awareness and the style and pattern of language.

10 Eve Merriam, *Rainbow Writings*, Atheneum.

Making the Story your own/a building process

Story Structure	Formula tales reveal their structure readily. Among the easiest to recognize are *cumulative* ("This is the house that Jack Built"); *sequential* ("Burnie's Hill" . . . What's in there? Gold and money. Where's my share? etc.); *recurring* ("A Spooky Story" . . . In a dark dark house there's a dark dark room etc.); *quest* ("The Old Woman and the Rice Thief" — a story which is quite circular in shape.)
Character Awareness	Leland Jacobs in a speech about how story lives in character provided a useful set of questions which I think stress awareness of character:

Who? (what character traits should be revealed?)
Who is where? (is the character central to the action?)
Who is when? (what kind of world does the character inhabit?)
Who wants what? (what motivates the character?)
What is who doing about what is wanted? (how are relationships with others important?)
How does who come out in the end?

Style and Pattern of Language	Good language engages imagination and conveys a sense of atmosphere. A love of sound is indispensible to the story-teller. The sound and rhythm of the words are often all part of their meaning. Each story directs us through its words to employ certain tone of voice, and to explore the full range of sound and silences which the story offers.

Keeping these building blocks in mind, what follows is an example of how the building of a story might be accomplished. A Congolese folktale will be the basis of our work:

THE BAMBOO TOWER

This story is an old Congolese version of the tale of the tower of Babel. The same story is found among the Bakongo and the Baluba.

The Lendu are very stupid people, say the Alur. One night as they gazed at the stars, they suddenly arrived at a very important conclusion, so they ran and communicated it to their king: 'We have realized that all those lights up there must prove that it is a prosperous country, in which many people can afford to keep their fires burning all night. We would therefore advise Your Majesty to build a tower up to the sky so that we can go and learn from those people.'

The king ordered that thousands of bamboo poles be cut, and hauled up to the highest hill in his realm. The first poles were dug into the ground, and cross-beams were tied to them with lianas. On top of this structure further storeys were erected, with diagonal poles and transverse beams for reinforcement. The king kept control of progress on top so that he rose up with every new storey. He wanted to be the first to set foot on the sky.

The chief minister, Ledza, was in charge at the bottom end. He directed the transportation of supplies. After nine months he noticed that the bamboo poles at the bottom were beginning to rot. The whole structure was beginning to sway unsteadily. With great courage and perseverance, minister Ledza climbed up all the stairs and ladders that had been constructed in those nine months, to see the king and warn him that his tower was tottering. The king merely said: 'Ledza, you are a liar, go back!' He could not be convinced that something had to be done, as he was constantly looking up at the sky, expecting all the time to reach it with the next storey. 'Go back to your duties, don't bother me with the problems of the earth, don't you see I am trying to meet God?'

The minister Ledza gave up, climbed down and ran away just in time. The whole tower tottered and collapsed in one terrifying crash, ndundu! All the builders perished and only the minister Ledza escaped.

Today there is still a lake on Mount Ju, surrounded by bamboo. It bears witness to the lack of intelligence of the Lendu people, according to the Alur.

from *Myths and Legends of the Congo*
Jan Knappert

Learning the Plot:

I believe it is important in the early stages to distance yourself from the language of the story in order that your own language might be brought into play. Try to jot down a very brief outline of the story as a beginning. Such an outline might look like this:

1. Members of the Lendu tribe believing the stars in the sky to be the fires of a prosperous king, urge their king to build a tower, which will enable contact to be made.

2. The king orders bamboo to be cut and a tower begins to rise from the highest hill in the land.
3. In order to be first to greet the sky tribe, the king stays atop the tower as it rises.
4. Supervision of the tower building rests with chief minister, Ledza, who after nine months labor, notices that the base poles of the tower have begun to rot.
5. Ledza climbs the swaying tower and tries to persuade the king to come down and abandon the plan.
6. Convinced that it is only a matter of a few more storeys until he will meet God, the king ignores Ledza's plea and dismisses him.
7. No sooner has Ledza reached the ground when the tower collapses. Enormous casualties are suffered by the Lendu tribe.
8. Today, a forest of bamboo bears witness to the scheme of the ancient Lendu.

Use your outline or the one here and study it briefly. Now, without looking at the outline, try to tell the story in your own words.

Here are three sample openings from retellings made by individuals who worked from their own outlines.

(a) "It was cold. Bitter cold. The people of the Lendu tribe had never experienced such cold. Their suffering was great. Already many of the aged and young babies had perished from it.

'We shall surely all die unless something can be done' the people cried.

Their king gazed hopelessly towards the heavens and then he exclaimed, 'I have noticed that the tribe which inhabits the land above us have many fires which burn throughout the night. Surely a people who can afford to keep fires going throughout the night must enjoy prosperity that can be shared with us. We must try to reach them and ask for help.' "

(b) "It has been said that the Lendu were a foolish people. It has been said that the Lendu lacked the sense to properly conduct their own affairs. But I ask you do you have the courage of the Lendu? Do you have the will to try to make your dreams come true or do you walk always with your eyes down fearing that you will bear witness to the greatness of others?

The Lendu were dreamers and the Lendu followed their dreams. Let me tell you about them."

(c) "It can not be said that the people of the Lendu tribe were the most brilliant whom ever lived, but on the whole they lived a quiet existence and seemed reasonably satisfied with their achievements.

There was a king to lead these people and he was not one who was given to extravagant schemes or grandiose design. And there was a chief minister, Ledza, to give him wise counsel. But a sudden turn of events marked the lives of these people for all time and the situation began like this."

Each approach is quite exciting. The pattern of the story has not been lost, but the tale has been altered to suit the teller.

Once you can tell the story from your outline, go back to the source and reread to determine if there are any significant details which have been omitted. Repeat the story in your own words adding those details which you deem important.

Creating Characters:

Reread the source material for a third time and give close attention to the characters. What dilemmas are they experiencing? How might they feel at various points in the narrative. Focus on one of the central characters and retell the story employing a first-person narrative style. If you wish, invent a character who might have been present during the event and tell the story through the eyes of that individual.

This a good way to stimulate thinking about the story; not only about its shape, but about relationships, motives and responses of characters. In addition it is a splendid way to free up the telling of a story.

Here are some openings created by participants at a workshop. The range of possibilities has been well illustrated.

(a) "I knew it was a fool idea the moment I heard it, but I've worked for the king long enough to know that when he makes up his mind to do something he's going to pursue it. What got him going this time concerned his stargazing and the sorry state of his coffers. . . ."

(b) "My name is Ledza, chief minister to the King of the Lendu tribe. My responsibilities have until recently been well within my ability to manage, but I fear now that I am in a situation which has gotten out of hand."

(c) "The first light of day has not yet dawned yet already my husband has returned to his labors. The torches of the workers form a ribbon of orange along the road leading to the great tower of the Lendu.

You see our king has taken the decision to build this tower to reach the prosperous tribe that inhabits the skies. Each evening we gaze with envy upon their campfires, shivering in the dark as we nurse the few embers which we are permitted. Fuel here is scarce and our king wishes to consult with the powerful sky tribe but to tell you the truth all of this scares me very much. My husband does not let on, but I know he too is filled with fear."

Telling the story from the point of view of another character in the story or an invented character, offers many interesting building possibilities. It is also a good way to test what you already remember about the story.

You might also consider the intent of the teller when you shape the story in this way. If you go back to the source material for a moment you will notice that the teller announces the intent of the story from the top. This tale is told in order to make fun of another tribe. That alone gives us interesting clues about how the story can be told.

Considering the teller and the teller's intent makes a wide range of variations available to you in terms of building the story in your own way. For example, if the story is told by a descendent of Chief Minister, Ledza, perhaps what emerges is a kind of hero tale. If the story is recalled by a tribesperson of the Lendu, the intent might be to deliver a cautionary tale about the folly of past leaders.

I know of storytellers who will gather together many versions of a story, painstakingly piecing together a word from that story, a turn of phrase from another story, until they have come up with a version they can claim as their own.

Varying the narrative style can also give you some unique and personal moments to add to the tale in order to make it truly yours.

Adding Details:

Return to the source material again and search for any important turns-of-phrase or words which give that story its own special sound. The word "lianas" might be one you wish to retain for example.

Retell the story again and try to picture every moment as you tell it. Are there details of sound, sight, smell, touch which you can add to enrich your telling?

Finally return to the source material one last time and study the opening and the closing.

I find it useful to memorize the opening and closing of a story. The impression you create when you start and when you finish are crucial. A bit of raggedness in the middle won't matter much, but an uncertain start or a muddled conclusion don't make for a satisfying listening experience.

Perhaps now you could tell the story to another person or to a group. This is when storytelling takes on the real excitement; for even though you know what you are going to do, until you interact with an audience you have no way of knowing how the story will turn out. For it is in the telling of the tale that so much of the shaping and learning about the story will take place. As you live in and through that story in your telling your listeners join you as co-creators. Together you react and respond to each other's signalling and the story unfolds as if it is being born for the first time.

The more you tell the story of course, the more you will be able to shape and reshape it until you find exactly what you want. There are also many other editing possibilities you might like to attempt such as:

— transposing from one historical context to another (*Do Not Open* by Brinton Turkle is a splendid example of a retelling of "The Fisherman and the Bottle" from A Thousand and One Arabian Nights)

— rearranging plot incidents (possibly starting in the middle and using flashback techniques)

— converting narration to dialogue

— condensing certain aspects of the story

— elaborating parts of the story or the roles of certain characters

— adding or deleting characters

— compressing the entire story

Although the preceding methods will work for any story you might wish to learn, it is especially well suited to material from the oral tradition. There are no definitive versions of folk literature and you should feel free to add your voice to the long list of voices which have continued to make and remake that tale.

In his introduction to *Italian Folktales*, Italo Calvino makes this point succinctly:

"The tale is not beautiful if nothing is added to it . . . . in other words its value consists in what is woven and rewoven into it. I too have thought of myself as a link in the anonymous chain without end by which folktales are handed down, links that are never merely instruments or passive transmittions but . . . and here the proverb meets Benedetto Croces' theory about popular poetry . . . its real 'authors'."

If you choose to tell an authored tale you may not feel comfortable taking as many liberties with the text. If your desire is to reproduce the work with a fair degree of accuracy then you might find it useful to chart the piece.

As an example of how this might be done Leon Garfield's retelling of the Old Testament story of the Tower of Babel follows:

KING NIMROD'S TOWER

There was a boy in Babylon who found a dog. It was a jumping, whooping, whirling, biting baby of a dog; and it had no friends. The boy called it "Snap", because it snapped; and the dog called him "Wuf!" because that was all it could say.

"I'll take you home with me," said the boy, "if you learn how to behave."

The dog bit his shoe; and whooped like anything.

"But I'll leave you here in the fields if you don't learn to behave."

The dog bit his trousers; and whooped again.

And all the brickmakers, carpenters, stone-workers, architects and surveyors who were working in the fields, laughed till they were told to stop laughing and get on with their work.

King Nimrod was building a tower. It was to be as high as heaven. The spot had been chosen, the stone fetched, the clay dug and the bricks baked. Ten thousand workmen fetched and carried, fetched and carried, and did as they were told.

"Look!" said the boy to the dog.

"And try to learn something."

"Hurry!" shouted the foremen.

"Hurry along there!"

And the workmen hurried along.

"Lift!" shouted the foremen.

"All together now — lift!"

And the workmen lifted.

"Sit!" shouted the boy to the dog. "Sit down, sir!"

The dog bit his sleeve and tore it; and whooped and whirled away.

It was a stupid dog. Its head was as thick as porridge, and its feet were like plates of mud. It would never learn to behave.

"King Nimrod will be walking into heaven," said the boy, "before I can take you back to Babylon, to sleep beside my bed."

King Nimrod's tower was growing fast. With ropes and hoists and cranes and ladders, it rose on a sweep of pillars and stairs. It was a mile round at the bottom, and already it was half an hour high. King Nimrod came to see it; and the ten thousand workmen stood to attention, one upon each of ten thousand steps. He climbed to the top and looked up at the sky, where heaven was waiting behind the clouds.

"God save King Nimrod!" everyone shouted together; and threw up their hats and handkerchiefs and dinner-bundles, till the tower looked like a tree with blossoms tossed up in the wind. "God save the King!"

King Nimrod shook his head and smiled. Soon he would be as high as heaven, and on a level with God.

"King Nimrod will save God," he said. "If God learns to behave."

There was a crack of lightning and a rumble of thunder; and the King said: "See! God is frightened. He is shaking in His shoes!"

"Bow down!" shouted the foremen. "Bow down to King Nimrod the Great!"

And all ten thousand workmen bowed down as low as dust.

"Down!" shouted the boy to the dog. "Down, sir, down!"

The dog bit his shirt and pranced and danced away.

"King Nimrod will be having supper with the angels," said the boy, "before I can take you back to Babylon, to sleep beside my bed."

Higher and higher rose the tower, till the workmen toiled in the clouds. Eagles stole their sandwiches, and rainbows painted their shirts.

"Stay at work!" shouted the foremen. "Stay at work or King Nimrod will stop your pay!"

And the ten thousand stayed hard at work; with bricks and mortar and heavy stones.

"Stay!" shouted the boy to the dog. "Stay or I'll stop your dinner!"

The dog jumped up and tore his collar; and whooped and whirled away.

"King Nimrod will be wearing God's dressing-gown and slippers," said the boy, "before I can take you back to Babylon, to sleep beside my bed."

And that was exactly what the angels said to God, who was watching the boy and the dog and not minding King Nimrod in the least.

"My slippers? My dressing-gown?" said God. "That cannot be."

"Behold, O Lord!" said the angels. "The tower is rising fast. Strike it down while there is still time!"

"But if it falls," said God, "the boy and the dog will be sure to perish under all those bricks and stones."

"Then what is to be done?" asked the angels. "How else is King Nimrod to be kept in his place?"

"How many miles to Babylon?" asked God.

"Three score miles and ten."

"Can I get there by candlelight?" asked God.

"Yes, and back again!"

So the angels lighted a candle and God went down into the fields of Babylon, where the foremen shouted and the workmen jumped and obeyed.

"Heave!"

And they all heaved.

"Lift!"

And they all lifted.

"Pull!"

And they all pulled.

Then God smiled and crossed His fingers on every tongue.

"Heave!" shouted the foremen.

And they all lifted.

"Pull!" shouted the foremen.

And they all pushed.

"Lift!" shouted the foreman.

Some pushed, some heaved, and some just sat and scratched their heads.

"What is happening?" shouted the foremen. "The tower will never get built!"

The workmen stared.

"What was that he said?"

"It sounded like, I must get a haircut!"

"No — no! It was, will you come to dinner tonight?"

"Never! He said his mother had a new dress!"

"Nonsense! He said, my feet are killing me!"

"You must be deaf! I heard it plain as anything. He said, is it time to go home yet?"

In the twinkling of an eye, and without a single lesson, they were all talking in languages they had never talked before! In Swedish, German, Spanish, Hebrew, Greek, Latin and Japanese . . . though to each and every one, it sounded like plain double-Dutch!

In vain the foremen shouted; in vain King Nimrod raged! The workmen heaved bricks where they should have put statues, and dug holes where they should have built stairs. In vain the foremen threatened; in vain King Nimrod stormed.

Nobody could understand them any more. And worse! The workmen couldn't understand each other, so they just downed tools and left.

They left the tower, they left the fields of Babylon, and wandered far and wide. Soon the great tower stood alone, crusted all over with pillars and piped with stairs, like an unfinished pie in the sky.

King Nimrod walked in the fields, as miserable as sin.

"My tower!" he wept. "My beautiful tower that was to have reached heaven! Alas! No more!"

But he could not even understand himself; and he drifted away like the dust. The boy and the dog were left all alone.

"Sit!" said the boy to his dog. "I only want to be your friend."

And the dog sat.

"Stand up!" said the boy to his dog. "I only want to take you home."

And the dog stood up.

"Good!" said the boy. "Now I can take you back to Babylon, and you can sleep beside my bed!"

So they went.

"How did it happen?" marveled the angels. "At last!"

"Because My Kingdom of Heaven is better reached," said God, "by a bridge than by a tower."

As you can see, the story presents an interesting learning challenge. In order to begin charting, the story has been divided into six episodes. Also included in the chart are sequences of words and phrases which might be preserved.

King Nimrod's Tower

EPISODE	OUTLINE FOR EACH EPISODE	WORDS AND PHRASES
One:	Boy meets and attempts to tame dog Segment ends: "get on with their work".	"jumping, whirling, whooping, biting baby"
Two:	Details about preparation for construction of tower and the marshalling of the laborers. Segment ends: "King Nimrod will be walking into heaven before I can take you back to Babylon to sleep beside my bed."	"fetched and carried" "rose on a sweep of pillars and stairs"
Three:	Progress on the tower is reported and Nimrod comes to inspect. Segment ends: "King Nimrod will be having supper with the angels before I can take you back to Babylon to sleep beside my bed."	"tower looked like a tree with blossoms tossed up in the wind"
Four:	Workers toil among the clouds. Segment ends: "King Nimrod will be wearing God's dressing gown and slippers before I can take you back to Babylon to sleep beside my bed."	"stop your pay" "stop your dinner"
Five:	God is goaded into action by the angels. Segment ends: "Soon the tower stood alone."	"Behold O Lord! kept in his place repetition 'in vain' "
Six:	King Nimrod makes his exit, leaving the boy and the dog alone to end of story.	"crusted over with pillars and piped with stairs like an unfinished pie in the sky" "My beautiful tower . . . Alas no more."

Once the story has been charted, certain structural features are obvious. The story operates very much like a windshield wiper sweeping first to the boy and the dog then to the tower construction. This back and forth pattern becomes a very useful device for keeping track of the story.

As I began to outline each episode, I was suddenly aware of the beautiful bridging between episodes provided by the three repeated sequences beginning "King Nimrod will be . . . and so on."

Now I had three pillars with which to anchor myself and to keep track of where I was in the story. My first building blocks were laid, adding the surface features would be reasonably easy.

With the structural features of the story in hand, attention to character and language could follow.

In taking on a story it is necessary for me to move back and forth between the world of the story and the personal imagery of my own memories, experiences and dreams.

I must see that story in my imagination. I must hear the voices of the characters speaking. I must identify with how the characters are thinking and feeling. I must have some idea of what that story is saying. Having done that, the story is part of me and I am part of it; the language flows freely.

I think it is this personal involvement in the story that marks the dividing line between telling a story and reading a story. With the text in front of me I am leaning more to what is in front of my eyes. Without that text, I must drop down behind my eyes to find the images I need to put the story across.

Once a strong sense of a story's setting and a keen awareness of the attitudes, feelings and concerns of the characters has been built, it is time to revisit the text to seek out significant details, beautiful words, recurring expressions and a general overall feeling for the language patterns appropriate to the story.

Each story has its own sound. If the storyteller is not sensitive to that sound, I feel that the special aura that story radiates will be lost. Of course the time spent on thinking about the characters and their motives, actions and feelings will help to capture the tone of that story, but there are word sounds that may not belong to that story and there will definitely be word sounds that do.

Words and phrases that I very much wanted to preserve in order to achieve the proper sound of the story were listed on the right side of the chart.

I can't imagine telling this story without echoes of the King James version of the Old Testament ringing in my ears. Colloquialisms don't belong with the word patterns of this story. Can you possibly hear the boy saying to the dog, "Jeez Wuf, knock it off!" I think not.

After each telling of the story, I go back to my source and listen to the story again until I am satisfied that my rendering of the story carries the sounds and rhythms of language that serve it best.

I have tried to stress that the bringing together of the story and the personal imagery of the teller are central to storytelling. Personalizing the story gives it the sincerity and conviction that make the experience truly memorable for the listener.

Storyteller Diane Wolkstein said of storytelling in Haiti, that where the community knows its body of literature, the storyteller must bring to the telling of a familiar tale, a fresh approach. The rules for storytelling in that community are simple, she explained, you must not tamper with the meaning of the story and you must not change the ending, otherwise you are expected to be very imaginative in your treatment of the story.

I cannot think of better advice.

CHAPTER FOUR

And This Is the Way I Tell It

*"As usual he (Stanley) was full of explanations for everything.
'This is a special place for telling stories in,' he announced, in
front of a huge, round building with a notice outside saying
Royal Albert Hall.*

*'There was this great King called Albert Hall who was
better at telling stories than anyone else, which is why he was
made King and he used to tell his stories to thousands of
people in here, that's why its got so many seats inside.' 'And
once,' he went on, his eye caught by writing scrawled in big
letters on some boarding outside — SPURS RULE O.K. —?
'once he had a terrible battle with this person called Spurs
who came and said he was even better at telling stories and
they fought for three days and three nights on that bit of
grass there on the other side of the road and at the end, King
Albert Hall threw this Spurs person into that lake there. . . .'*

'Belt up, Stanley,' said Ned."

from *The Voyage of QV 66*
Penelope Lively[10]

Telling a story is an intensely personal experience. There are a few
general principles to remember, but by and large each of us must
assess our individual strengths and capitalize on them. Unlike the
imaginary battle between King Albert Hall and that Spurs person to
determine who was the better storyteller, I wish to approach this
chapter by pointing out that what I have to say here is what has
worked for me. It may not always fit into your frame of reference
and you might be in disagreement. I accept that!

10 Ibid.

I have kept a record of questions that continue to be put to me about storytelling.

Here are the questions and my answers to them.

QUESTION: Do you wear a costume or play an instrument when you tell stories? How important are props with your stories?

ANSWER: I sometimes think people look a little disappointed when I tell them that I never wear a costume to tell stories, nor do I play an instrument. I seldom use any props. All of this strikes me as a bit too theatrical. Theatrical I am not, but dramatic, definitely yes.

Sometimes when telling a story I create the voices of the characters and employ the full range of emotions open to them. I'm not talking about getting in the way of the story by placing myself at the center of things, but I am talking about letting the natural dramatic aspects of the story come to the surface.

Today, we tell stories in parks, around campfires, in public libraries and in schools to children who have grown up with television and for whom close encounters with stories shared by interested adults are not the rule. Television has caused us to adopt different patterns of thinking about stories through rapid cuts, flash backs, flash forwards and commercial messages coming at rapid-fire pace. Attending to an oral tale requires getting used to if its not been part of your life. For these reasons alone, if we are to establish communication with these listeners and capture their attention, we need the best dramatic readers and storytellers in the world. If that involves movement or vocal or body sound effects, then so be it! I repeat, however, that the dramatization must be that which occurs naturally, just as the voice we use should be that which is used in natural conversation and not one pitched an octave higher with a sing-song delivery.

QUESTION: Do you use the same voice style for every story?

ANSWER: Each story will demand a different vocal treatment. A story's needs should become apparent as you prepare it and consider what it means to you. Some stories will require an easy conversational tone; some will require quiet, suspenseful telling; others will demand a mock-serious style.

You will find that in telling the story, your most exciting discoveries will be made. The more opportunities you have to tell a story, the more this becomes apparent. I told one story for nearly a year before it began to feel right. Some stories take a while to understand.

Often, a story will require slightly different vocal interpretation depending on the age and experience of the listeners. Leila Berg provides a useful comment:

"There is one story here, Little Dog Turpie, that is loved unreservedly by all the children I tell it to, except one; and when I tell it to him, I have to tell it in a warm laughing way, that tells him that he and I are together on this, and we'll see the little old man and the little old woman and Little Dog Turpie safely through."

from *Folktales*
Leila Berg

QUESTION: Do you ask questions after you tell a story?

ANSWER: No. My aim in telling stories is to provide my listeners with an imaginative experience. There are no questions I could possibly pose that would be relevant even if I did want to.

I am much more interested in natural responses to a story, which people make on a voluntary basis. Some of the most exciting learning about a story for me has come in these exchanges afterwards. Sometimes this experience is enlightening, sometimes moving and occasionally humbling.

Once, a middle-aged gentleman came up to me to comment on a story I had told. He had liked the story, but was puzzled by his feelings about it. "Had I omitted some detail?" he inquired. I was extremely embarrassed because I had been telling a Scottish fairytale and had deliberately "softened" some of the more violent bits. Obviously, I had communicated my discomfort and concern. My tampering had resulted in the experience being less than whole for that gentleman. I confessed to my error and walked away much wiser.

Should you ever find yourself tempted to do likewise, it might be better for you to seek another story.

QUESTION: What are some of the greatest difficulties you face when storytelling?

ANSWER: I once shared a week of storytelling at Artpark with the great American storyteller, Brother Blue. Each day as we left the storytelling theater, Blue would say "Storytelling is hard work. It's plain hard work!"

Both outdoors and indoors it is indeed hard work. There are some things you can do however to make things easier on yourself.

Outdoor storytelling is a great challenge. Shifting crowds and extraneous noise can be the bane of a storyteller's existence. I have had to stop my story completely to accommodate jet aircraft, trucks, police sirens and once I was attacked by a dog who got excited about the story. When working outdoors, I try to look for a spot where movement behind me is eliminated and where I can practically stand in the crowd's lap. You must be clearly visible to everyone and I often hold my arms out at a forty-five degree angle from my body and request that no one sit outside the area bordered by my reach. Outdoors, you must be persistent and not give up or complain. If interrupted, pause, then plunge right in again.

At the Hans Christian Andersen Storyhour in Central Park, New York, the storyteller stands at the base of the steps leading up to the statue of the beloved teller of tales. Usually, one or two officials from the Hans Christian Andersen Storytelling Committee unobtrusively ensure that no one climbs onto the statue during the storytelling. Anyone, child or adult, who creates a disturbance or lights up any smoking material is given the cold, fishy eye or even a verbal reprimand. Telling a story on a summer Saturday morning in this great metropolitan park is an exceptional experience.

Telling stories indoors is usually a bit easier, but there can be difficulties. I have been in many schools where finding the right place to listen takes some careful thought.

Place yourself where you can be easily seen and where the lighting on you is clear, not shadowy. Stand away from windows so that the listeners are not facing into the light. Similarly place yourself in a spot that isn't too busy in the background (such as a display of bright paintings). If it is necessary to stand to be seen, stand. If not, you might be more comfortable sitting down. Avoid standing or sitting behind a desk, lectern or some other obstruction. It puts a barrier between you and your listeners. Once, in order to be seen in a university amphitheatre, I stood on a table. I don't recommend this, but do whatever is necessary to give yourself the best chance with the group you're facing.

QUESTION: Do you plan exactly what stories you will tell in a session and in what order they will be told?

ANSWER: If I am doing a specific program I plan meticulously what stories I will tell and I order them carefully. In addition, I list some back-up choices. All of this is written down on a piece of paper I keep in my pocket. However, this is no indication of how the session will go.

Communicating with a group is an exhilarating and creative experience. You the storyteller know your role, you know what you're going to do and you know how you're going about it, but you can never tell how it is going to turn out. You must be prepared to be flexible — even if you have only one story — and handle whatever behavior the listeners throw up at you.

It's not unlike a football game where the quarterback calls the play and the team lines up. As the quarterback approaches the center, he scans the opposing defense. If he anticipates that the defense has read the play, he quickly calls "an audible" and the team prepares to go with the new plan. So it is with storytelling. You face the group, glance around at the listeners, take note of the signs and signals and try to understand the situation. Often in that split second before I open my mouth to speak, I have made the decision to abandon the story I wanted to tell and have gone with another.

QUESTION: Could you be more specific about what would cause you to change your mind about telling a story and what you would do about it?

ANSWER: If I see a group which appears restless and seems indifferent to the experience, I will try to jolly them along a bit. One of my favorite ploys with a group like this is to use a lot of rhetorical questions in order to build an awareness of how the story is unfolding, to encourage anticipation and to focus the listening. (For example, Have you ever met anyone like this? How do you think you would feel at this point? and so on.) This is a very risky thing to do however, for if you don't work deep within the context of the story you can quickly lose control. I love the give-and-take of communicating with a crowd and if you can employ such a device to get the crowd with you it can be extremely effective.

I have worked with groups where the listening didn't become sharpened until after one or two stories. Sometimes it takes that long to settle a group.

Another device I will use to focus a group is to select a story that involves the audience in the chanting of a refrain or the singing of a chorus. With an especially restless group, such a strategy gives the storyteller badly needed breaks in order to compose himself or herself and an opportunity to observe the group carefully and adjust the telling as necessary.

QUESTION: What do you consider to be one of the most important assets a storyteller, working in a public sense, can have?

Answer: Energy! You must have the kind of energy that enables you to reach out, without shouting or straining your throat, and touch every person in the group, no matter how large, with your voice. Your desire to tell a story you love and your confidence in your own preparation and ability to tell the story your way will be all you need to summon that energy.

The energy of the group is important too. A lethargic, unresponsive group can leave you dragging. A keen, responsive group that hangs on to every word and practically breathes in unison can buoy you up and actually leave you feeling full of vigor.

With a difficult group, I establish my foundation of support pretty quickly. I look for the shining eyes and the glowing countenances of the individuals who are with me. There is always one, usually more than one. Although I maintain strong eye contact with the whole group and try even harder to carry the story to them, my eyes flick regularly back and forth to those supporters who are helping to carry me.

Question: How do you deal with interruptions to the story?

Answer: If you mean interruption as in a listener speaking out, usually to ask a question, I answer directly by incorporating that question and my answer into the context of the story. For example, "You ask why the boy allowed himself to be caught by the giant? He's under a very powerful spell do you remember? And so powerful was that spell. . ." and so on.

Once, in a park, a drunk wandered into a storytelling session. He stood, swaying gently, trying to figure out what was going on. His presence was creating tension in the audience. Then he did what everyone was afraid he would do. He shouted out a comment over top of my voice. I kept going. He shouted again. The group was becoming quite agitated. Before anything else could happen I replied directly to him, not skipping a moment of the story. He nodded and kept quiet for the rest of the story, then he shambled off.

Even the keenest listener can be lost to an unanticipated interruption. Often, everything you have built in terms of a story can be blown up in front of you and there's little you can do about it.

One time I was telling a story to a large group of teachers in a school gym. I was approaching the climax of the story when, suddenly, the public address system boomed on and an authorative voice rasped out a list of license numbers for illegally parked cars. I couldn't believe what happened next. People leapt to their feet, chairs scraped and banged and high heels clicked across the wooden floors. When the confusion died, I quickly resumed the story and mustering all the confidence that I could, I finished it. In that kind of situation all you can do is keep your composure and finish the job in the most dignified manner you can.

Sometimes, a storyteller can lose a group with too much idle chatter. If it's necessary to introduce a story, it should be brief and to the point. I usually prefer to start right in on a story with no introduction and chat later about it with those who are interested.

QUESTION: How does the classroom teacher build and maintain a repertoire of stories when the opportunity to tell any given story occurs about once a year.

ANSWER: This is indeed a problem, but it can be overcome. My early repertoire was heavily dependent on short pieces similar to those collected by Alvin Schwartz in his book *Whoppers*[11], nursery rhymes, and cumulative and chain tales. Gradually I began to collect variations of the tales I already knew since they were easy to absorb. Of course I read to the class a great deal. Surprisingly, a few years later I could tell *those* stories pretty accurately without the book. For the most part, a story read or told to the class was also further extended by dramatic exploration. Drama was an excellent way to become more deeply aware of the story and its relatives.

I would also advise keeping a journal on the work done with stories. I write where and when I told a story and how it was received in my journal. I have included some random jottings from my journals (there are many now) which I still refer to.

Sample Journal Entries:

Journal entry — *a fall fair*
> *The space is noisy; the crowd constantly coming and going. Adults bring children close to the storyteller then retreat and hang back on the fringes. Recommend use of a microphone next year. Stories don't work here without it.*

Journal entry — *The Spider's Palace* (Hughes)
> *Finding the right voice for this story is important. Opening can be a bit terrifying. Strive for an offhand or matter-of-fact tone.*

---

11 Alvin Schwartz, *Whoppers*, Lippincott.

Journal Entry — *I Can Squash Elephants* (Carrick)
Attempt to rework and revise the ending. At the moment it seems anti-climactic. Bring story to an end after "frog's" closing speech.

Journal Entry — *A Christmas Program*
All stories were very powerful. Audience was very quiet and reflective at conclusion. Give listeners more time to "come back" with such material before going on to the next story.

Journal Entry — *Opening Day — Artpark Summer of '81*
Today's session had to be the hardest ever. The audience consisted of sixty pre-schoolers, a summer day camp for pre-teens, several families, a dog and a bus load of "seniors" — all eating box lunches.

A garbage truck smashed bottles for the first fifteen minutes over at the theater and a training jet made six thundering passes.

A steady, rapid delivery saved the day along with lots of participation work.

QUESTION: What advice do you have for people getting started at this kind of thing?

ANSWER: I am convinced that storytelling is an art form which can be practiced by anyone who has the desire.

I have watched professional storytellers tell stories that, like so many TV situation comedies, carry no weight. They have performed in a slick polished style that has brought a crowd to its feet applauding.

I have also watched beginners tell a story in a faltering, even stumbling, manner that has reached deep into the hearts and minds of the listeners and left them feeling complete satisfaction.

Choosing a story that will help the listener to understand the richness of life and the complexities of being human, and telling it with sincerity are absolutely basic as far as I am concerned. Of course delivery is important too, but the first two conditions are of prime importance.

Many beginners tend to rush through their material. Be aware of this and try to start slowly and make the most of every word and every sound. Clarity of speech is important. Another skill to develop is the use of silence. The pause is an excellent device to help build suspense and to permit your listeners to savor the pleasures of anticipation.

I cannot give you foolproof guidelines for the use of the pause, but I can encourage you to let your story work for you. Where are the suspenseful bits, which will benefit from slow build-up with pauses injected at critical points? Which passages should be skipped over quickly and where should we go slowly? In most instances, careful reading of the material will furnish you with clues.

QUESTION: I worry that my vocabulary isn't good enough for telling a story without the book in front of me. What can I do to overcome this?

ANSWER: I think that if you can relax, make the most of the words you have, enjoy them, and make everything happen as you say them, then there is little to be concerned about. As you learn more stories you soon discover that many expressions and word patterns will transfer almost automatically from one story to the next.

QUESTION: When you encounter difficult, foreign or obsolete words in folktales, do you substitute for them when working with young children?

ANSWER: I don't ever substitute for the words of a story. They are part of the story and its style and unless they interfere directly with meaning, I offer no explanations. Quite frequently, repeated use of words in questions within the context of the story will suffice to make their meanings understood. I am convinced that words not understood have a charm and magic of their own which children enjoy. I find it exciting to puzzle and ponder over strange words, to listen to their sound and guess at their sense.

If I think a word is going to block significant meaning, I simply explain it within the context of the story without interrupting the flow. Often young children will ask in the middle of a story for explanation of a word. Without any fuss I tell them and the story remains unbroken.

QUESTION: How important are the voices in a story? Do you have to characterize vocally in order to tell the story well?

ANSWER: Here again, you must do what comes naturally to you. I never deliberately set out to do voice characterizations, yet my inner ear continually guides me on this. I have heard storytellers set out to characterize then lose track of which voice sounds like what. Your awareness of the emotions and thoughts of a character at any given time in the story are probably a better approach to characterization than being concerned about the sound per se.

QUESTION: I can't do dialects very well. What would you advise?

Answer: I can't do them either, so I don't make the attempt. Try to tell the story in a manner comfortable to you. There's nothing worse than listening to someone attempt dialects and not pull them off.

Question: My voice isn't particularly interesting to listen to. Do you have any tips?

Answer: The voice we have is the voice we must use. If you think you have special problems, it might be a good idea to take a few voice lessons. Many people often have problems with breath control and learning to breathe effectively relieves the throat of considerable strain. It has been my experience that it is possible to use the voice with greater flexibility. A relaxed natural manner, a feeling for words and a willingness to experiment with interpretation will go a long way to improving your vocal work.

Listening to all manner of stories, songs, plays, conversations, disputes and languages helps too. Here are some recordings of poets and storytellers that you might like to investigate.

Barrow Collection Argo PLP1072
Magic Egg The Barrow Poets Argo ZSW511
Islands of the Moon The Barrow Poets A.S.W. ASW6001
Canadada: Four Horsemen Griffen House
Call-And-Response Ella Jenkins Scholastic SC7638
Sense and Nonsense (Peggy Ashcroft, Martin Best, Edward Flower) Argo ZSW532
Hans Christian Andersen in Central Park Stories told by Diane Wolkstein Weston Woods WW713
Tales To Grow On The Folktellers Weston Woods
Stories told by Laura Simms Weston Woods
Tales from an Irish Hearth Alice Kane The Storytellers School of Toronto†

Question: How do you involve listeners in the story?

Answer: I involve listeners in the story in three ways (not all at once, necessarily). The simplest most natural way is to invite everyone to chime in with you on repetitions, refrains, chants or songs. Children will do this naturally with stories they love to hear again and again. If there is already a little sound motif in the story, listeners can be easily persuaded to help you handle it.

---

†Manufactured and distributed by: The Storytellers School of Toronto, 412A College Street, Toronto, Ontario, M5T 1T3.

Sometimes I will ask an audience to help me heighten the suspense of a fun story by providing sound effects. Before telling the story, I catalog the needs. For example we might need the sound of wind on a stormy night or the creaking of a shutter on rusty hinges or raindrops on tin roof. Once we have agreed upon and rehearsed the sounds, I tell the story. The listeners have to be alert for the clues that indicate what sounds are to be made when. This is an especially good focusing activity for a group that needs a release of energy.

The third way I involve listeners is to give out roles. These can be formalized roles in a story where one or two characters utter a repetitive line with some regularity. Once the group understands how the story is working and have caught on to the clues about who speaks when, all you have to do is point and pause and they usually respond. For example in *Burnie's Hill* which we used earlier, I give the answer to the questions posed by the group.

There are also opportunities for informal roles, often in crowd scenes where individual comments can be ad libbed by the listeners on cue from the storyteller. For example, "I understand that the step-mother and the stepsister made Little Sister do all the work inside the house and all the work outside the house. I'll bet you neighbors know what some of those tasks were . . ."

QUESTION: What new ideas do you have for us to develop our own stories?

ANSWER: Probably the simplest stories you can tell are ones about your own childhood. They may be ones centered around holiday celebrations or special friends; often relationships with other members of the family. Children like to hear stories about the lives of their parents or teachers when they were little.

Russell Hoban's book *La Corona and the Tin Frog* reminded me that a child's toys can become the subject matter for invented stories. I keep a small box filled with unusual little wind up toys that I find on my travels. At the moment, the box contains an orange crocodile whose jaws open and close once it is wound, a green frog with a baby frog riding piggy-back behind and a little yellow Pac man-type creature, also a wind-up. They are a wonderful group to build stories around.

A well-known story such as *The Three Bears* can also be set in the familiar environs of your own neighborhood. The local jug milk store, the park and so on. Local figures, the neighborhood cat, and the children themselves, can be incorporated into the tale.

Some nursery rhymes are sufficiently open-ended to permit an extension of the tale. Others adapt nicely to the creation of additional verses. For example, "On Saturday night I lost my wife" could be extended to what happened on Sunday night, Monday night, Tuesday night and so on.

Another method of creating stories focuses on the sounds and rhythms of words hooked together thematically. I call this vocal jazz.

Vocal jazz celebrates words — words which began as sounds as well as the sounds words contain and the pattern of sounds words make when strung together.

Patterns can be made using words from many sources. A word music composition on "The World of Soup" might begin with the assembling of a soup's ingredients, proceed to a rendering of exciting soup names (Alibaba Noodle Cream, Cold Creme Curry) and end with the final slurp of a satisfied soup eater.

The following word music composition was built up around the idea of "talk".

First of all the synonyms for talk which could be remembered were listed. The list produced such words as, blabber, blither, drone, yammer, bellow, chat, jabber, prattle, announce, exclaim, quibble, gossip, yap, declaim, drawl, expound.

Next, categories of talk were considered. From the example of the Doris Day/Rock Hudson film *Pillow Talk*, bus talk, gutter talk, staffroom talk, locker room talk, street talk, double talk, hand talk, baby talk, back talk, shop talk, big talk, in-talk, bilateral talk, beans talk (a small pun), over-the-back-fence talk, behind-closed-doors-talk and under-the-table talk.

According to the situation in which talk is featured, there are certain appropriate forms it takes. In this regard the lists included, innuendo, scolding, monologue, dialogue, parley, lecture, sermon, eulogy, debate, soliloquy, interview, forum, diatribe, quarrel, *tête-à-tête*, proposition, jamboree, *coroboree* (Australian) *chataqua* (North American Indian).

To conclude, all the expressions used to bring talk to an end were brought forth such as, pipe down, silence, hold your tongue, knock it off, quiet, "hush yo mo", ssh!, cool it, seal your lips, stuff it, clam up, stifle yourself, stow the gab, *fermez la bouche*, shush yourself, put a plug in it, on hold.

From all the raw material on the lists, the development of the jazz composition commenced. Mainly, the effects desired were interesting sounds and patterns of sounds. Here is one example of a communal composition.

ALL:	TALK!	(followed by a babbling of voices lasting about ten seconds)
ALL:	TALK!	
Solo 1:	Bellow	
Solo 2:	Yap	(to be spoken
Solo 3:	Jabber	in cheerleader
Solo 4:	Yammer	fashion)

Note:
The instruction here had been to select four words from the first list and arrange them in an interesting sound pattern. Sound quality is all important.

All:	bellow, yap, jabber, yammer	
Solo 5:	Chat	
Solo 6:	Prattle	
Solo 7:	Blither	
Solo 8:	Blather	
All:	chat, prattle, blither, blather	Note: This sequence was built
Group A:	(chant) shop talk, shop talk etc	up cumulatively,
Group B:	(chant) double talk, double talk etc.	by adding groups
Group C:	(chant) over-the-back-fence talk etc.	one, two, three, four, one at a
Group D:	(chant) under-the-table talk etc.	time.
All:	Chat aqua, soliloquy, innuendo	
	Chat aqua, soliloquy, innuendo	
	Chat aqua, soliloquy, innuendo	
	(chorus continues but fades under as solos are called over)	
Solo 9:	*Fermez la bouche!*	
Solo 10:	Hold your tongue!	
Solo 11:	Stifle yourself!	
Solo 12:	Knock it off!	
All:	CUT!	

In bringing this word music to life, many ancient storytelling techniques have been employed. These include, call and response (echo), chiming-in, and competitive chanting. In addition, the experience has included word building, word association, gaming with words, playing with synonym, homonym, antonym and experimentation with onomatopoeia. It has also been a vehicle for speaking aloud with expression, with ease and with joy.

The activity is easily adapted to work with any age of child or adult. The experimenting with concept, with teasing it out into its constituent parts then creating a simple framework on which to hang the words is at the center.

For example, a word music piece about Trains might involve expressions commonly associated with trains (for example, tickets please! all aboard!) sounds of trains (clickety can, clickety can, whooo!) names of famous "ghost trains" which are no longer with us (Newfie Bullet, Flying Scotsman, Cannonball Express), call letters of well known railroads (Via, B.&O., Atcheson Topeka and Sante Fe) Canadian place names with unusual sounds (Wawa, Come-By-Chance) and two or three great railroad songs.

A quick look at some of Donald Crews' concept books such as *Boats* and *Rain* or Ted Harris's *Northern Alphabet* yield additional ideas for word music composition.

Here is a composition that was built from a nursery rhyme. I have often built this in connection with a storytelling workshop in order to feature story patterns from the oral tradition and to help the members of a group to recall story experiences from their own folk heritage.

Group A: I'll tell you a story about Jackanory
(chants   And now my story's begun.
twice)   I'll tell you another about
            Jack and his brother
            And now my story is done

Group B: (begin when group A reaches "begun")
(chants   I'll tell you a story about Jackanory
twice)   And now my story's begun.
            I'll tell you another about
            Jack and his brother
            And now my story is done

Group A: (chant)	Again and Again Again and Again Again and Again (fade and down)
Group B: (chant)	In a dark dark house There's a dark dark stair Down the dark dark stair There's a dark dark cellar Down the dark dark cellar There's a dark dark box In the dark dark box There's a *Ghost!*
Solo 1:	SCREAM!
Group B: (chant)	On and on, on and on On and on, on and on (fade and down)
Group A: (chant)	Pete and repete sat on a fence Pete fell off Who was left?
Group B:	REPETE!
Group A:	Pete and repete sat on a fence Pete fell off (fade and down)
Group B: (up and)	BACK AND FORTH BACK AND FORTH BACK AND FORTH
Group A:	What's your name?
Group B:	Mary Jane
Group A:	Where do you live?
Group B:	Cabbage lane
Group A:	What's your number?
Group B:	Bread and cucumber!

Group A: (singing)	The grand old Duke of York He had ten thousand men He marched them up to the top of a hill And marched them down again (keep repeating)
Group B: (singing)	London Bridge is falling down, falling down etc.
Group A:	(fade out Grand Old Duke of York and chant softly in and over) And now my story is done And now my story is done
Group B:	(fade out London Bridge chant in and up) And now my story is done And now my story is done
All:	And now my story is DONE!

In creating this piece, the group has worked with infinity stories (Pete and Repete), stories with repetitive sequences (In a dark dark house) question and answer structures which are featured in many old ballads, folk songs and playground lore and stories sung in varying movement patterns (London Bridge — arch, Grand Old Duke — advancing/retreating lines). Although only a few stories have been employed in the composition, many more have been recalled, told and chuckled over. Occasionally little rhymes and stories are told in languages other than English to produce unusual sound textures.

QUESTION: How do you integrate music, movement and drama into storytelling?

ANSWER: The vocal jazz demonstrated in the previous example is one of the most effective methods I know for creating an impressionistic story, which explores sound and rhythm and song and has potential for movement.

Perhaps one of the most interesting methods lies in the traditional singing and drama games. All of us have participated naturally in such drama games as London Bridge Is Falling Down, Ring-A-

Ring-O-Roses and Old Roger Is Dead and Laid in His Grave. One of the best books on the subject I know is *Step It Down* by Bessie Jones and Bessie Lomax Hawes. Here are wonderful stories in dance, mime, drama and song. Music notation is provided, but for those who learn best by ear there is a companion record.

Children's Games in Street and Playground (Oxford) by Iona and Peter Opie is another excellent source of this kind of material.

QUESTION: What is the difference between acting and story-telling?

ANSWER: Acting takes place in front of your eyes. Storytelling happens behind them.

QUESTION: What type of stories do young children enjoy hearing best?

ANSWER: I can give you no better answer than the one Elizabeth Cook gives in *The Ordinary and the Fabulous* (Cambridge):

"Stories that lead to doing things are all the more attractive to children who are active rather than passive creatures. Myths and fairytales provide an unusually abundant choice of things to do. Largely because they are archetypal and anonymous (in quality, if not in provenance), they will stand reinterpretation in many forms without losing their character. They can be recreated by children not only in words but in drama, in mime, in dance and in painting. Action in them is not fussy, and lends itself to qualitative expression in the movements of the human body and in the shapes and colors of non-figurative painting."

CHAPTER FIVE

Reading Stories to Children

Matt decided to skip B for bone. *In the night he had thought of a better way.*

"This book isn't a treaty," he began. "It's a story. It's about a man who gets shipwrecked on a desert island. I'll read some of it out loud to show you."

He opened Robinson Crusoe *at the first page and began to read.*

I was born in the year 1632,
in the city of York. . . .

He stopped. He remembered suddenly how the first time he had tried to read this book he had found that first page so dull he had come close to giving up right there. He had better skip the beginning and get on with the story if he wanted to catch Attean's attention.

"I'll read the part about the storm at sea," he said.

He had read the book so many times that he knew exactly where to find the right page. Taking a deep breath, as though he were struggling in the water himself, he chose the page where Robinson Crusoe was dashed from the lifeboat and swallowed up in the sea.

Nothing can describe the confusion of thought which I felt when I sunk into the water, for though I swam very well, yet I could not deliver myself from the waves so as to draw breath . . . for I saw the sea come after me as high as a great bill, and as furious as an enemy. . . .

from *The Sign of the Beaver*,
Elizabeth George Speare[12]

12 Elizabeth George Speare, *The Sign of the Beaver*, Houghton Mifflin Company.

Like the storyteller who works from memory, the reader of stories must also bring thoughts, feelings, characters and ideas to life. The reader of stories must also be able to visualize what is happening and transmit this to the listener.

When you read aloud, there is a physical object, the book, to contend with as well as language constructions. The level of sophistication of the printed word will also demand keen listening on the part of your audience. Anyone who picks up a book to read aloud without some preparation runs the risk of wallowing into an experience which will be no joy for either reader or listener.

When reading aloud, the task is so much more than speaking print. Knowing when to turn the page of a picture book in order to build suspense or keep pace with the flow of the text can make an enormous difference. And even the best story can benefit from a little pruning in a read aloud situation.

One reason we read to children is to extend their reading range and strengthen their ability to take in complex language. Children's capacity to take in language is generally ahead of their ability to read; even so it will be necessary to pass over some unimportant details, shorten lengthy passages of description or asides and perhaps tell some segments in your own words.

Practising the story out loud will also help reveal the qualities of sound and rhythm it possesses and give some indication of the places to pause in a way that the eye can't detect. At the same time the vocal treatment to be used can be considered. Should delivery be matter-of-fact? Would some voice characterization add more life?

Much of the appeal of folktale lies in its ability to capture interest quickly by plunging the listener into an action-packed situation. Look for stories to read aloud that do the same.

Notice how quickly we are pulled into the events of Philippa Pearce's *The Battle of Bubble and Squeak* (Andre Deutsch):

> *"The middle of the night, and everyone in the house asleep.*
> *Everyone? Then what was that noise?*
> *Creak! and then, after a pause, Creak! And then, Creak!*
> *And then, Creak! As regular as clockwork — but was this*
> *just clockwork? Behind the creaking, the lesser sound of some*
> *delicate tool working on metal.*
> *The girls heard nothing. Amy Parker was so young that*
> *nothing ever disturbed her sleep. Peggy, too, slept normally.*

*Sid Parker, their brother, heard in his dreams. He was the
eldest by a little, and slept more lightly. Besides, he had been
half expecting to hear something. He had dreaded to hear it.
He came swimming up from the depths of his dreams to the
surface: now he was wide awake, listening. Creak! he heard;
and then Creak! . . . . Creak! . . . . Creak!*

Sid broke into a sweat as he listened.

*And their mother? Mrs. Sparrow heard it. The noise woke
her, as the crying of her children would have woken her.*

*But this was someone else's job. She nudged her husband,
the children's stepfather. She nudged and nudged until Bill
Sparrow stirred, groaned. He had been dreaming of the
garden: mostly marrows, and runner beans that towered over
their apple tree. . . .*

'Bill!' she whispered. 'Come on! Wake up!'

'Yes,' he said. 'Just a minute, and I'll do that.'

'Listen!'

Creak! and then, Creak! And then, Creak!

'Can't you hear it?'

'Yes.'

'What is it?'

'I don't know.'

'But it's in the house!'

'Yes it is.'

'Downstairs!'

'Yes.'

'Bill, what are you going to do about it?'

The brisk, suspense-filled dialogue, the short sentences and the
vivid images make this easy don't they? "What happens next?" has
been deftly established. Not all stories hook the listener this quickly.
Some brisk dramatic reading on the part of the reader might be
necessary for several chapters until the story takes hold. In a one-on-
one situation this is often less difficult than when trying to read to a
group. In group situations especially, the time spent in getting
prepared to read will pay off.

Once a story has been selected and a simple plan for oral interpretation considered, the actual reading should commence slowly at
first then quicken as it becomes apparent that the listeners have slip-
ped into the story world. It is important to look up from the book

frequently and to note the signals which the listeners are sending. A furrowed brow, an indifferent look, slouching posture all indicate that adjustments to your style may be required.

Choosing a Read Aloud Story:

There are some books that read aloud better than others. Haunt your local public library and school library and garner all the advice you can from the children's librarians on what works well out loud. These titles have worked especially well for many:

Mr. Gumpy's Outing, John Burningham, Holt, Rinehart & Winston.

A delightful cumulative tale with lots of repetition for young listeners to become involved in. A great favorite with young children.

Funnybones, Janet and Allan Ahlberg, Heinemann.

A simple repetitive story pattern becomes the vehicle for the hilarious nighttime adventures of two Mutt- and Jeff-type skeletons. A wonderful book for out loud performance. There are singing bits too.

Where the Wild Things Are, Maurice Sendak, Harper & Row.

The story of Max and his adventure with the Wild Things who "roared their terrible roars and gnashed their terrible teeth" has become a modern children's classic. Don't overlook Sendak's *In the Night Kitchen* or *Outside Over There*.

The Little Girl and the Tiny Doll, Edward and Aingelda Ardizzone, Puffin.

One day a tiny doll was thrown into a supermarket freezer by her owner. Thus begins this gentle story about a lonely, frightened doll and a little girl who sets out to help her.

Follow Me!, Mordecai Gerstein, Morrow.

In addition to a hilarious vaudeville-type routine, which reads aloud brilliantly, this story also introduces colors simply and effectively.

Mary Alice Operator Number Nine, James Marshall, Little Brown.

Mary Alice took her work as telephone operator seriously and she was good at it. Then one day she came down with a cold and had to leave her post. Who could possibly fill in for her? If replaced, would Boss Chicken ever give her back her job? An amusing read aloud.

My Name Is Emily, Morse and Emily Hamilton, Greenwillow.

An unusually warm and comforting story about a little girl who has run away from home and then is welcomed back into the family through a fast moving game of words.

How the Loon Lost Her Voice, Anne Cameron, Harbour.

A northwest coast Indian myth telling how Loon and other creatures tried to reclaim daylight from evil spirits who had hidden it behind a wall of ice.

The Amazing Bone, William Steig, Farrar, Straus and Giroux.

In William Steig's delightful stories, his main characters often undergo fantastic transformations, which trigger a cliffhanger adventure. Pearl Pig in this story finds a talking bone and the action erupts.

How Tom Beat Captain Najork and His Hired Sportsmen, Russell Hoban, Atheneum.

Aunt Fidget Wonkham Strong wore an iron hat and took no nonsense from anyone. Her practical joker nephew, Tom, needed to be taught a lesson she decided. In the wild and wacky tests he was put to, Tom's fooling around paid off handsomely.

Babylon, Jill Paton Walsh, Andre Deutsch.

Up the railway viaduct, away from their dirty streets, Dulcie and her playmates enter an imaginary world which triggers for her friends, memories of their home in Jamaica. But Dulcie was born in London. She has no such memories. A sensitive and satisfying read.

All the King's Horses, Michael Foreman, Hamish Hamilton.

A modern fairy tale in which a wrestling princess takes on all comers in a tale of great hilarity and action.

Sleeping Ugly, Jane Yolen, Coward McCann.

A modern fairy tale in which a nasty princess locks horns with a seemingly inept fairy. Fast, funny and fabulous.

The Ghost Horse of the Mounties, sean o huigin, Black Moss Press.

Set in western Canada, this story, based on a true incident, takes us back to the early days of the Northwest Mounted Police.

Other excellent read aloud books not to be missed.

I Was a Second Grade Werewolf, Daniel Pinkwater, Dutton.

Has Anybody Seen My Umbrella, Max Ferguson, Scholastic-TAB.

Little Bear, Else Holmelund Minarik, Harper & Row.

John Brown, Rose and the Midnight Cat, Jenny Wagner, Bradbury.

Oliver Hyde's Dishcloth Concert, Richard Kennedy, Atlantic Little Brown.

Thomas' Snowsuit, Robert Munsch, Annick Press.

George and Martha, James Marshall, Houghton Mifflin.

The Wild Washerwomen, John Yeoman, Puffin.

Foolish Rabbit's Big Mistake, Rafe Martin/Ed Young (illus.), Putnam.

Duffy and the Devil, Harve and Margot Zemach, Farrar, Straus and Giroux.

The Frog Who Drank the Waters of the World, Patricia Montgomery Newton, Atheneum.

Thistle, Walter Wangerin, Harper & Row.

The Story of Mrs. Lovewright and Purless Her Cat, Lore Segal, Knopf.

Ways Forward:

In read-aloud situations, adults are often amazed at children's ability to fill in, word for word, parts of a well-loved tale or to correct an errant reader who has omitted a well-loved portion of a story.

Children are usually willing partners in the telling of a story. Not only is the experience a pleasurable one for them, but it is an opportunity to enhance listening, speaking and language awareness. As the child waits for his or her part, not only are listening skills increased, but the child's sense of what constitutes a story is sharpened.

An important skill for becoming an independent reader is anticipation. The suggestions that follow encourage not only anticipation, but participation. If children are to become lifelong readers, enjoyment of stories and response to stories is a must.

(a) Single-sitting Books

Picture books, folk and fairy tales, and short stories can generally be read in a single session and still permit time for talk in and around the story, as well as a chance to examine the illustrations and do some co-operative reading aloud.

Many stories of these kinds contain a repeated phrase, simple pattern of dialogue or refrain, which children will chant spontaneously.

Once a child is familiar with the way the story is working, the reader can pause in anticipation of the phrase, verse, question or answer and let the child *chime in*. The formula tales listed in chapter two all encourage listener participation. Also look for:

Could Be Worse!,   James Stevenson,   Greenwillow.
The Elephant and the Bad Baby,   Elfrida Vipont,   Puffin.
Each Peach Pear Plum,   Janet and Allan Ahlberg,   Viking.
Yummers!,   James Marshall,   Houghton Mifflin.
Millions of Cats,   Wanda Gag,   Coward McCann.

The following stories all contain a great deal of repetition. They are easily followed by children as the established bits are repeated again and again.

Mortimer,   Robert Munsch,   Annick Press.
The Clay Pot Boy,   Cynthia Jamieson,   Coward McCann.
The Troublesome Pig,   Priscilla Lamont,   Crown.
At Mary Bloom's,   Aliki,   Greenwillow.
Joseph Had a Little Overcoat,   Simms Taback,   Parents.

Some stories involve extensive dialogue between two characters. Once children are familiar with the material, roles can be taken and the story read co-operatively.

For example: In Eric Carle's *The Grouchy Ladybug* (Crowell), a belligerent ladybug tries to pick a series of fights with creatures of various size and classification. In each case, the ladybug addresses her adversaries with the words:

"Want to fight?/Oh you're not big enough."

The child can take the lady bug's repetitive speech while the adult reader handles narration and the direct responses of the various creatures.

*"At seven o'clock
it saw a stag
beetle.
'Hey you.' said the
grouchy ladybug:
'Want to fight?'
'If you insist.'
said the stag
beetle,*

*opening its jaws.
'Oh you're not
big enough.'
said the grouchy
lady bug
and flew off."*

As you proceed, page size and typography change with each encounter. How this will be accommodated in the oral interpretation is the fun of the experience.

Another good source for this kind of experience is *A Flea Story* by Leo Lionni. This little fantasy is a kind of two-character play starring an adventurous flea who wants to step out and see the world and his or her flea pal who is somewhat of a "stick-in-the-mud."

They set out on an adventure, which is viewed as terribly exciting by the one flea and terribly vexing by the other.

The direct speech of each insect is enclosed in a boldly outlined balloon. Each outline is a different color. After one or two practice runs, child and adult can engage in some lively dramatic oral reading. How will the colors of the balloon borders be incorporated into your interpretation?

Here are a few additional titles that might also be explored:

Ask Mr. Bear, Marjorie Flack, Macmillan.
Going to Squintum's, Jennifer Westwood, Dial.
Red Is Best, Stinson/Lewis, Annick.
Little Fox Goes to the End of the World, Ann Tompert/John Wallner (illus.), Crown.
Peace at Last, Jill Murphy, Dial.

A similar kind of pairs reading can be explored with question and answer stories.

Karla Kuskin's *Roar and More* can provide some lively entertainment.

Each double spread in this old favorite contains a verse about an animal on the left hand side and a picture of the creature on the right hand side. For example, on the left of the first spread we are told:

"If a lion comes to visit
Don't open your door
Just firmly ask "What is it?"
And listen to him roar."

On the right side of the spread is a picture of the "jungle king" himself.

When the page turns, however, the entire second spread is filled with the word R O A R in bold black lettering.

The reader can handle the text and the listener can respond to the word and picture clues by supplying the appropriate sound when the page is turned; a simply delightful shared reading experience for a young child and adult reader.

Other books which offer this kind of opportunity include:

Have You Seen My Duckling?,   Nancy Tafuri,   Greenwillow.
Can You Moo?,   Althea,   Dinosaur.
Where's Spot?,   Eric Hill,   Putnam.
Would You Rather?,   John Burningham,   Crowell.
Smile For Auntie,   Diane Paterson,   Dial.

(b) Excerpts from Longer Works

Often I find myself in situations where I will be reading to a group one time only. If I am trying to interest them in reading a selection for themselves or just providing them with a rewarding listening experience, I will sometimes select a series of key passages from a book, which focus on one of the story's themes or characters. In this book, I have included a series of excerpts from *The Voyage of QV 66* that comment on the nature and art of storytelling and reading aloud. Taken together, they provide an interesting strand which runs through the novel.

If this seems too difficult, try to lift little stories from longer works, which even out of the larger context, can stand on their own as stories.

You might look to these novels for the following examples:

(N.B. The titles of the excerpts are my own with the exception of "Blackbirds" and "Hello Bluebird")
"The Hand", p. 43-45, *The Hollow Land*, Jane Gardam, Greenwillow.
"What a Great Day!", p. 136-140, *The Wheel on the School*, Meindert deJong, Harper and Row.
"You Are the Night and I Have Caught You!", p. 136-140, *Zeely*, Virginia Hamilton, Macmillan.
"Blackbirds", p. 19-27, *Salt River Times*, William Mayne, Greenwillow.
"Hello Bluebird," p. 40-43, *That Scatterbrain Booky*, Bernice Thurman Hunter, Scholastic.

(c) Serialization

Reading a chapter a day until the book is finished is a common way of handling longer works. If there is any drawback to this approach it is that the reading can stretch on too long causing significant details of the story to be lost. Where there are considerable time gaps between readings, serialization might be a poor choice.

There are, however, many books which adapt well to this approach. Undoubtedly one of the best of these is *The Iron Man* by Ted Hughes. Each of the five chapters can be read in about forty minutes, thus in a week the book can be completed. It is of course, possible to condense the reading time of a longer work by combining the reading with some telling in your own words.

Susan Hirschman, senior editor and vice president of Greenwillow Publishing House, says that she is convinced that a skilled reader can capture children's interest with a stirring rendition of the telephone directory. I believe her.

We owe it to our children to select books that will stretch imaginations and keep alive the "read to me" spirit. Such books often include those which the children might not find for themselves, but can be introduced by an interested adult. They will be books that arouse curiosity and help children to discover new relationships and gain new insights. They will be books that pose difficult questions, perhaps, and push the listeners into thought-provoking situations. They will be books that feature a wide variety of styles of writing as well as subject matter.

Here is a baker's dozen of books that meet the above criteria. In addition, they are well suited to serialization:

The Adventures of the Little Wooden Horse,   Ursula Moray Williams,   Puffin.
A Year and a Day,   William Mayne,   Puffin.
The Sea Egg,   Lucy Boston,   Harcourt Brace Jovanovich.
The Dreamtime,   Henry Treece,   Hodder and Stoughton.
Sunshine Island Moonshine Baby,   Clare Cherrington,   Collins.
The Saga of Erik the Viking,   Terry Jones,   Schocken.
The Ship that Flew,   Hilda Lewis,   Oxford.
The Piemakers,   Helen Cresswell,   Macmillan.
Mrs. Frisby and the Rats of Nimh,   Robert O'Brien,   Atheneum.
Go Saddle the Sea,   Joan Aiken,   Jonathan Cape.
Abel's Island,   William Steig,   Farrar, Straus & Giroux.
The Whale People,   Roderick Haig-Brown,   Collins.
Maiden Crown,   Meghan Collins,   Houghton Mifflin.

There are many possibilities when choosing books to read

aloud, but the following categories offer some additional ways of exploring and finding material. In particular I would like to draw attention to picture books for the older reader, reinterpretation of vintage works and books which feature the exploration of language.

Picture Books and the Older Reader:

Many years ago as a teacher of drama, I was made aware of issues, often political or sociological, which were being raised in modern picture books. Far from being books which addressed the needs and interests of young children, these books explored territory which was of greater significance to those nine and ten years of age and older.

Children today are influenced by the mass media, in particular television. The fleeting nature of so much which passes before their eyes, however, leaves little opportunity for exploration and reflection. The modern picture book represents a significant source for teachers or parents in challenging children to think, discuss, play out and look again.

Of particular interest to me is the opportunity which these books provide for bringing together children of varying ages and reading ability for shared activity and as a stimulus for further reading and viewing.

In addition to challenging and sophisticated subject matter, the widely varying styles of expression provide countless opportunities for comparison and comment. For example, Russell Hoban's modern satirical fable, *The Dancing Tigers* could be read alongside Douglas Davis' retelling of a traditional African myth, *The Lion's Tail*, Jan Wahl's modern short story *Tiger Watch* and Anthony Browne's surreal *Bear Goes to Town*. Together, these picture books and illustrated stories present a fascinating array of perspectives on the co-existence of mankind and various species of the animal kingdom. Much reflection and discussion are made possible by this exciting group. Some other examples which illustrate widely varying styles of expression and subject matter are:

The Garden of Abdul Gasazi, Chris Van Allsburg, Houghton Mifflin.
Future Story, Fiona French, Bedrick.
Sammy Streetsinger, Charles Keeping, Oxford/Merrimack (dist.).
Outside Over There, Maurice Sendak, Harper & Row.

The King's Fountain, Lloyd Alexander, Dutton.
The Nose Tree, Warwick Hutton, Atheneum.
The Hockey Sweater, Roch Carrier/Sheldon Cohen (illus.) Tundra.
Gidju, Percy Trezise / Dick Roughsey, Collins.
Chin Chiang and the Dragon's Dance, Ian Wallace, Atheneum.
The Voyage of Prince Fuji, Jenny Thorne, Macmillan.
The Enchanted Caribou, Elizabeth Cleaver, Atheneum.
Ytek and the Arctic Orchid, Garrett Hewitt/Heather Woodall, Vanguard.

Reinterpretation of Vintage Works:

Artists in all fields have proven that reinterpretation of an older work can be extremely innovative. Often an older work possesses a charm or archetypal power, which lends itself to being reworked or translated into contemporary terms. Sometimes, it is our appreciation of the genre, shape or achievements of the original, which causes writers and artists to want to work within the framework.

In many ways these reinterpretations introduce a new generation to classic stories which they might not otherwise hear about.

Two examples of reinterpretation which deserve mention: Leon Garfield's *King Nimrod's Tower*, which appears in this book and is a superb example of a new story which has been invested with the feelings of the original.

Do Not Open by Brinton Turkle (Dutton) is a brilliant transposition of a story from one historical context (*A Thousand and One Arabian Nights* "The Fisherman and the Bottle") to another (a twentieth century coastal setting). Also look for:

Latki and the Lightning Lizard, Betty Baker, Macmillan.
The Boy Who Would Be a Hero, Marjorie Lewis, Coward McCann.
The King of the Pipers, Peter Elwell, Macmillan.
City of Gold, Peter Dickinson, Gollanz.
The Writing on the Wall, Garfield/Bragg, Lothrop.
The King in the Garden, Garfield/Bragg, Lothrop.
My Mother Sends Her Wisdom, Louise McClenathan, Morrow.
Jim and the Beanstalk, Raymond Briggs, Coward McCann.

During the past two decades, there has been a vast outpouring of traditional fairytales resplendent in their new images. The stunning visual treatments given many of these old tales has caused criticism from some quarters to be leveled at illustrators who are accused of indulging themselves at the expense of children's imaginations. While there is some merit in this argument, there have been many especially fine publications featuring illustrations which stretch the viewer's perspective of the story. Some outstanding examples are:

Hansel and Gretel,   Anthony Browne,   Julia Macrae.
Yeh-Shen,   Ai-Ling Louie/Ed Young (Illus.),   Philomel.
Snow White,   Nancy Ekholm Burkert,   Farrar, Straus & Giroux.
The Wild Swans,   Hans Christian Andersen/Angela Barrett (illus.), Benn.
The Sleeping Beauty,   Warwick Hutton, Atheneum.
The Selfish Giant,   Oscar Wilde/Lisbeth Zwerger (illus.),   Picture Book Studio.
The Twelve Dancing Princesses,   Janet Lunn/Laszlo Gal (illus.) Methuen
The Little Mermaid,   Hans Christian Andersen/Margaret Maloney/ Laszlo Gal (illus.),   Methuen.

Books Which Feature the Exploration of Language:

Roar and More, Karla Kuskin/Harper & Row; *Once: A Lullaby*, bp nichol/Black Moss and *Clams Can't Sing*, James Stevenson/ Greenwillow all provide opportunities to play with the sounds of language. Another source of prolific experimentation is the alphabet. In the dozens of alphabet books, which have been published in recent years are some of the most innovative adventures with letters one could wish for. I doubt whether teaching the alphabet is nearly so important in these books as engaging the reader in a terrific visual and thought-provoking exercise. Try to find some of these as starting points for your own journey through the alphabets.

The Sonia Delaunay Alphabet   (color),   Sonia Delaunay, Crowell.
The Most Amazing Hide and Seek Alphabet,   (typography/3-dimensional),   Robert Crowther,   Kestrel/Viking.
All in the Woodland Early,   (music),   Jane Yolen,   Collins.
A Peaceable Kingdom (rhythm and rhyme),   Alice and Martin Provensen,   Viking.
Ape in a Cape (verse), Fritz Eichenberg, Harcourt Brace Jovanovich.

Albert B. Cub and Zebra (story), Anne Rockwell, Crowell.
ah! belle cité/a beautiful city abc, Stéphane Poulin, Tundra.

Undoubtedly, the most exciting play with language occurs with poetry. On the whole, poetry receives little attention, yet as a source of delight for child and adult it is unbeatable.

It is essential to offer a wide variety of styles and subject matter, but you can't go wrong if you begin with the enjoyment of rhythm. Fun words and fun rhymes powered by pulsating rhythms are a part of playground rituals and games and in poetry much of the pleasure of the unexplained mystery of unfamiliar names and strong rhythmic sounds.

> *Hominy, succotash, racoon, moose*
> *Succotash, racoon, moose, papoose.*
> *Racoon, moose, papoose, squash, skunk*
> *Moose, papoose, squash, skunk, chipmunk*
> *Papoose, squash, skunk, chipmunk, mukamuck*
> *Skunk, chipmunk, muckamuck, woodchuck.*[13]

Tongue twisters and nonsense verse, riddles and parodies, chants and songs are all good starting points especially because they encourage participation.

The following anthologies are excellent sources for this material:

Hop-Along Happily, Cynthia Mitchell, Heinemann.
Inky Pinky Ponky, Michael Rosen/Susanna Steele, Granada.
A House Is a House for Me, Mary Ann Hoberman, Viking.
Arm in Arm, Remy Charlip, Parents.
Auntie's Knitting a Baby, Lois Simmie, Western Producer Prairie Books.
Sally Go Round the Sun, Edith Fowke, McClelland and Stewart.
Mister Magnolia, Quentin Blake, Jonathan Cape/Merrimack (dist.).
Mother Goose Comes to Cable Street, Rosemary Stones/Andrew Mann, Kestrel.
Alligator Pie, Dennis Lee, Macmillan.
It's Raining, Said John Twaining, N.M. Bodecker, Atheneum.
Silly Verse for Kids, Spike Milligan, Puffin.
Roger Was a Razor Fish, Jill Bennett, Lothrop.

---

13 Charlotte Pomernatz, *If I Had a Paka*, Greenwillow.

The Young Puffin Book of Verse, Barbara Ireson, Puffin.
Don't Eat Spiders, Robert Heidbreder, Oxford.
Quips and Quirks, Clyde Watson, Crowell.

Children from eight to ten years of age are often fascinated by story poems that are slightly bizarre and touch upon taboo topics. I think that much of Shel Silverstein, Dennis Lee, sean o huigin and Michael Rosen's work appeals for this reason.

Some anthologies to consider are:

Magic Mirror and Other Poems for Children, Judith Nicholls, Faber.
Songs for My Dog and Other People, Max Fatchen, Puffin.
You Can't Catch Me!, Michael Rosen, Andre Deutsch.
The Puffin Book of Magic Verse, Charles Causley, Puffin.
Ducks and Dragons, Gene Kemp, Faber.
Sky in the Pie, Roger McGough, Kestrel.
A Light in the Attic, Shel Silverstein, Harper & Row.
Lizzy's Lion, Dennis Lee, Stoddart.
Well, you can imagine, sean o huigin, Black Moss.
The New Wind Has Wings, Mary Alice Downie and Barbara Robertson, Oxford University Press/Merrimack (dist.).

We can do no greater service to children than to create a nurturing environment where shared experiences with story is a regular occurrence. Under such circumstances, even children who are experiencing difficulty mastering reading skills seem to build and maintain positive attitudes towards stories, books and reading. These children enjoy stories, they relish old favorites, they look forward to new experiences with stories. In short, they acquire a genuine enthusiasm and love for literature.

CHAPTER SIX

Uncrating the Story:
Storytelling in the Classroom

*"The old woman had a huge bag full of earth on her back. It
was a certain kind of sandy earth. This is what they must
have in the lodge. The dancers must dance upon sandy earth.
The old woman held a digging tool in her hand. She turned
towards the south and pointed with her lips. It was like a
kiss, and she began to sing:*
  We have brought the earth.
  Now it is time to play;
  As old as I am, I still have the feeling of play.
  *That was the beginning of the Sun Dance . . . it was all
from Tai-me, you know, and it was a long time ago."*

(N. Scott Momaday)

Each February when the thought of another six to eight weeks of
winter seems impossible to bear, a local department store stages a
yearly sales promotion based on the notion of "uncrating the sun".

Suddenly it seems, images of wooden packing crates filled with
such goodies as warm sun rays, palm fronds and gentle southern
breezes spring up everywhere. Although I have never rushed off to
the store to bask in all these warmish thoughts, the idea of uncrating
all those wonderful sunny things has always filled me with a sense of
anticipation, expectation and wonder.

It is in connection with several articles on children as storytellers
in the classroom that these "uncrating images" emerged. The articles
emphasized children learning traditional tales in order to retell them

orally. The reworking of stories dominated the activity and little stress on personal interpretation and explorations was given. So much can be learned about a story orally, yet this was often passed over in favor of activities which involved research, charting, journal entries, writing fiction and reports, and reporting to the class. Where suggestions for oral activity did appear, the most frequently cited examples were choral speaking and dramatization.

I tried to think about child storytellers I had listened to in such settings. So often I sensed little of the child in the retellings. Oh they knew the story alright, but the experience struck me a little bit like oral painting by numbers. I longed for the storytellers to inform me about their insights into the story based on their own experience of it. I longed for the spontaneous informal style of their own personal narratives recounted gleefully with peers in the less formal setting of the schoolyard.

All this brought those packing crate images tumbling through my mind. Children like to retell and get things in the right order. They are curious about stories. What if our work with children and storytelling placed the emphasis on "uncrating the story", on finding stories inside the story, of exploring layers of meaning. Could that unpacking involve them in the anticipation, expectation and wonder that discovery brings? Might our work involve searching for clues, exploring questions and examining details by bringing the children's storymaking abilities to bear by creating extended opportunities for talk in and around the story.

Certainly, when adults and children get together around stories, the adult must become a co-explorer with the child; encouraging questioning, speculating, recalling of past experience and the building of personal discoveries in order to make conclusions about the work.

Ultimately I would hope that this pulling away of "the packing" would help children understand that a story is something you can shape to your own existing knowledge and that any time the story is revisited it can be remade again and again.

For the purposes of this chapter, the uncrating will be considered in two ways — celebrating the word and close reading.

Celebrate the Word:

Celebrate the word is about exploring the workings of words and sounds. It promotes responsiveness, sharing, and co-operation. In the process it develops good expressions and articulation as musicality, force, dynamics, volume enunciation and a wide range of expressive behaviors are practiced.

Call and Response Stories:

Among the simplest stories to tell are puns, catches, tongue twisters and tangletalk. All of these are easily found in collections of nursery rhymes and can be played out loud, in gamelike fashion.

Playing "follow the leader" with words is one of the earliest forms of storytelling. Call and response or echo tales are the more commonly known expressions to describe this form of storytelling.

The popular campfire story "We're going on a lion hunt" is a well-known example of this kind of storytelling. Actually almost any verse or story can be told this way; listeners merely repeat the lines of the storyteller, word for word. I look for selections with strong rhythm patterns, simple diction and fascinating sounds such as these skipping rhymes:

> Salome was a dancer and she danced the hootchie kootchie
> She shook her shimmy shoulder and she showed a bit too
>   much
> "Stop!" said King Herod, "You can't do that here!"
> Salome said, "Baloney!" And she kicked the chandelier.

> Had a little racing car
> Number 48
> Drove it to the c-o-r-n-e-r
> SLAMMED ON THE BRAKES
> Bumped into a lady
> Bumped into a man
> Bumped into a policeman
> Man o man

> Policeman caught me; went to jail
> All I got was gingerale.
> How many bottles did you get?

Chiming In:

Find infinity stories and invite the listeners to join in as soon as they understand how the story is working.

> Who put the overalls in Mrs. Murphy's chowder?
> Nobody answered so she hollered all the louder.

Father and Mother and Uncle John
Went to market one by one
Father fell off
Mother fell off
And Uncle John
Went on and on and on and on . . . . .

Just as games children play release the body and mind to explore and experience, playing with words releases the voice and imagination to explore the rhythms, sounds and meanings of language.

Sound Exploration:

Word play from the ancient play circle to the twentieth century playground has relied on either playing with meaning or playing with sound. The activities that follow encourage participants to become absorbed in the feel of words and to explore their voices.

Chanting:

A word's most distinctive characteristic is its sound. Exploring it is good fun. For example, the poem *Sink Song* yields numerous possibilities.

Chant the piece together out loud in call and response fashion. Chant it slowly in deep voices; chant it quickly with light voices; chant it with booming voices; chant it in a whisper.

SINK SONG

Scouring out the porridge pot,
  Round and round and round!
Out with all the scraith and scoopery.
Lift the eely ooly droopery,
Chase the glubbery slubbery gloopery
  Round and round and round!

Out with all the doleful dithery,
Ladle out the slimery slithery,
Hunt and catch the hithery thithery,
  Round and round and round!

Out with all the oobly gubbly,
On the stove it burns so bubbly,
Use the spoon and use it doubly
  Round and round and round!

J.A. Lindon

Have everyone claim a word whose sound he or she particularly likes. Have the group chant, in unison, their personal choices over and over softly. Alert the group to listen carefully to determine which sound or sounds predominate. Without any change in volume, challenge the group to join in with the sound they think predominates until the group that started chanting many different sounds is now chanting the same sound in unison. The activity requires great concentration. Each individual has to be prepared to give up his or her own sound in order to be part of the group.

Divide the large group into several smaller ones and have each group claim one word from the piece whose sound they would like to work with. First the group must create a three dimensional likeness of the sound or draw it with color and texture. Next the groups practise chanting the sound out loud. Its texture must be apparent through some combination of high and low pitch, soft or loud volume and fast or slow delivery. Bring all the groups together with their three dimensional representations, which are held high as the group makes its sound. Experiment with sound patterns, working on interesting combinations and juxtapositions of the groups.*

Here is a sound poem by Edwin Morgan. Decide how the words should be spoken to put across your ideas of what is happening. To speed up the process perhaps different lines could be given to groups or individuals. When the group has worked the piece all it cares to, listen to the Barrow Poets version on the album *Magic Egg* (Argo ZSW511).

THE LOCH NESS MONSTER'S SONG

Sssnnnwhuffffll?
Hnwhuffl hhnnwfl hnfl hfl?
Gdroblboblhobngbl gbl gl g g g g glbgl.
Drublhaflablhaflubhafgabhaflhafl fl fl - -
gm grawwwww grf grawf awfgm grraw gm.
Hovoplodok-doplodovok-plovodokot-doplodokosh?
Splgraw fok fok splgrafhatchgabrlgabrl fok splfok!
Zgra kra gka fok!
Grof grawff gahf?
Gombl mbl bl- -
blm plm,

* I am grateful to Jim Rahn for the development of this activity.

blm plm,
blm plm,
blp.

What meaning can be put across through the sound? Is the monster hungry, frightened, in love? (The poet says that the Loch Ness Monster comes to the surface, doesn't like what he sees and submerges.)

This is what Eve Merriam thought a "stuck horn" might sound like. Can the participants say it and make it sound like they think Eve Merriam wanted it to sound?

THE STUCK HORN

unmOOOOOOOOOOOOOOving
in glUUUUUUUUUUUUUUUUUUUUe
sunk in OOOOOOOOOOOOOOOOOOOze
snaggling in the same dragging
grOOOOOOOOOOOOOOOOOOOOOOOOOOOOOOOOOOOve
throw a bOOOOOOOOOOO or a shOOOOOOOOOOOe
gag it with a rag   bottle it   stopple it   pickle it
pinprick it   tickle it with a straw from a
brOOOOOOOOOOOOOOO OOOOOOOOOm
just when you think it will stop it
reneWWWWWWWWWWWWWWWWWWWWWWs
somebody please
dOOOOOOOOOOOOOOOOOOO
somethingsOOOOOOOOOOOOOOOOOOOOOOOOOOOn

Hold up a series of familiar objects one at a time. For example a hand bell, a cap pistol, a tambourine, a pair of chopsticks. Have the participants vocalize all the sounds they can think of for each object. Turn the sounds into words and record them.

When the vocalizing is finished, have the group sort and classify the lists of sound words. What will the classifications be? Using a pattern on which to hang the sound words, have the participants working in small groups, fit sound words to the pattern. (The limerick pattern works well, but others such as cinquain and so on may be just as useful.) Instruct the group that only words from the lists may be used. No articles, prepositions, conjunctions are allowed. When the group has constructed a pattern they can begin to give it voice.

Jabberwocky beware!

Hooking Words Together:

In the following activities, the object will be to tell a story or event using single words. The result will probably be more of a word pattern that creates an impression as opposed to a story with a beginning, middle and end.

Using the idea of lists, word patterns can be quickly and easily formed. For example if we make a list of boats we might come up with:

tug boat	laser
steam ship	cruiser
catamaran	Chinese Junk
and so on.	

Putting the words into pleasing arrangements and chanting them out loud until the sound is "right" would be a good first step. Varying the chanting techniques could be explored next. For example, call and response, or chant in skipping rhyme rhythm.

Word patterns can be sought in catalogues, advertisements, storybooks, poetry anthologies and best of all in cook books. Here is a *found list* from *Up To Low* by Brian Doyle (Groundwood).

MY FATHER'S ONION SANDWICH

2 huge Spanish onions	*salt*
fresh bread	*beer*
butter	*mayonnaise*

Cut the middle slice (1/2" thick) out of each onion. Throw the rest of both onions out in the yard.

Get a big loaf of fresh, hot, homemade bread from some farmer's wife whose dress smells like milk.

Cut 2 slices, (2" thick) from the centre of the loaf.

Save the rest of the bread for tomorrow's bread pudding.

Plaster the bread with butter.

Put on the onion slices.

Pour salt to her.

Get a beer and some mayonnaise.

Put lots of mayonnaise on the onion slices.

Close the sandwich and with the heel of your hand, press.

Eat.

ADVERTISEMENT – WORD PATTERN

1. Title:
   Weeds Weeds
   Weeds Weeds
   (chant 3 times)

2. solo
   repeat at least
   twice (check your
   yard and garden for)

3. chorus response to
   solo at least twice
   (Birds, bugs, and animals,
   too.)

4. solo: role call

5. have each animal
   weed taken as a solo
   After each solo have
   the whole group chant
   the word (call and
   response)

6. for ending, have half
   the group chant
   this (Around the garden)
   while other half does
   the title
   Weeds, weeds, weeds,
   weeds.
   Chant again and again
   getting softer and
   finally fading out.

Birds, bugs and animals, too

Check your yard and garden for foxglove, leopard's bane, bee balm, heron's bill, fleabane, butterfly bush, crane's bill, partridgeberry, larskpur, dragon's head, spiderwort, dogwood and horse chestnut.

And check the Garden Pages in Section 2 of the New York Times ... every Sunday ... for seasonal news, feature articles and advice about what you should or could be doing "Around the Garden."

The Garden Pages, Every Sunday, Section 2 of
The New York Times

Note how the captions and other words can be employed as well as the list of *critters*.

Once the piece has been interpreted orally, work can focus on the animals weeds' sound. Does the leopard's bane come across with sufficient snarl? Is fleabane spoken in a teeny tiny voice? How will the other birds, bugs and animals sound?

Here are some word patterns that tell a kind of story. Read them out loud together. Remember, each word is different, has its own way of being said. Try to get the exact meaning and feeling into the voice to tell the story. (Your voice should show what you think the sound feels like) Once you have familiarized yourselves vocally with the piece try to give it physical action, perhaps even work out the movement story that goes with the words.

Day peep
Day spring
Meridian
Mainday
Dayligone
Dimity
Dewfall
Gloaming
Dusk
Owlery

from Ounce Dice Trice
by Alastair Reid   Atlantic Little Brown

There are many other ways to hook words together. For example, sean o huigin includes a wonderful introduction to experimental poetry in his delightful book, *Well, you can imagine* (Black Moss Press).

Tracing Ritual Pattern:

How many miles to Babylon?
Three score miles and ten.
Can I get there by candlelight?
Yes and back again.

If your heels are nimble and light
You can get there by candlelight.

Traditional

This terse, tense little conversation represents another form of storytelling from the oral tradition. Drama games, which we have all played, are as much a part of folk art as song, dance and choral verse. Their *raison d'être* lies in the doing; in bringing people together to communicate; to feel and to enjoy the communion with other human beings.

Generally these games have only the simplest dance movements: advancing and retreating in lines, circling left or right or winding into the center, and passing under human arches. Some form of chant or song accompanies the movement; the rest is dramatic action for spontaneous improvisation is essential to the spirit of the activity.

Drama Games:

Drama games form part of the cultural heritage of all people. What children have preserved throughout the ages are the roots of primitive ceremonies of the ancients. The magic in the words, music and movements is universal and general. It comes from a time when the actions dramatized were the real actions of daily life. The business of love, politics, religion and warfare were all carried out in the form of social games. Indeed all cultural activities were social games enacted in the play circle. For a bookless society, this was the way to remember. Remnants from these times still abound in today's world. Antiphonal singing, impromptu versifying and contests are but a few examples.

Something in the hypnotic repetition, the sound of chanting, the fun of wordplay and the excitement in sudden shifts of scene lure us together and help us "to come to know the shape, sound and texture of other human beings."

Although specific words are given for the games that follow, they represent but one of many variations. In some cases, the words used in the past have been lost, only fragments remain. To these have been added other words from less distant times.

Participants might start to create other words, lines or verses, add bold gesture or create new movements. Such adaptation is the norm for the oral tradition in all times, in all cultures.

Call and response or chiming-in activities permit us to become vocally involved in story. In the following drama games, the feeling of the ancient play circle is recreated as participants join in, not only with voice, but with body.

DID YOU FEED MY COW?

"Did you feed my cow?"
   "Yes Mam!"
"Will you tell me how?"
   "Yes Mam!"
"Oh what did you give her?"
   "Corn an' hay."
"Oh what did you give her?"
   "Corn an' hay."

"Did you milk her good?"
   "Yes Mam!"
"Did you do like you should?"
   "Yes Mam!"
"Oh how did you milk her?"
   "Swish! Swish! Swish!"
"Oh how did you milk her?"
   "Swish! Swish! Swish!"

"Did that cow die?"
   "Yes Mam!"
"With a pain in her eye?"
   "Yes Mam!"
"Oh how did she die?"
   "Uh! Uh! Uh!"
"Oh how did she die?"
   "Uh! Uh! Uh!"

"Did the buzzards come?"
   "Yes Mam!"
"For to pick her bone?"
   "Yes Mam!"
"Oh how did they come?"
   "Flop! Flop! Flop!"
"Oh how did they come?"
   "Flop! Flop! Flop!"

Traditional

This call and response story can be told together with lots of movement, including the milking of cows and the swooping of buzzard wings.

This is a complete description of "Old Lady From Brewster" as played by Bessie Jones in her book *Step It Down*.

> There's an old lady from Brewster,
> She had two hens and a rooster,
> The rooster died, the old hen cried.
> "I can't lay eggs like I used to."
> Now, oh, Ma, you look so,
> And, oh, Pa, you look so.
> He said, "Who's been here since I been gone?"
> "Two little boys with the red cap on!"
> Hang them boys on a hickory stick,
> Papa's gonna parch them soon! Wham!

Pain in the head!	*Ranky tanky.*
Pain in the shoulder!	*Ranky tanky.*
Pain in the waist!	*Ranky tanky.*
Pain in the thigh!	*Ranky tanky.*
Pain in the knee!	*Ranky tanky.*
Pain in the leg!	*Ranky tanky.*
Pain in the feet!	*Ranky tanky.*
Pains all over me!	*Ranky tanky.*

MRS. JONES' COMMENTS:

"This is an old time game. Many people hear about me talkin' about it all the time, and it's from way back in slave, too. People would whip your children whenever they do wrong around their place. And they didn't have no mercy — they meant it. But this man had . . . three daughters and they all got old enough to take company and when they did, they had special company, because in those days girls went with boys that the parent say go with. And if they were pleased with them, then they went with them, without that, they didn't. And that boy would be responsible for the girl, so not all kind of boys didn't hang around the house. So this is what was done. This man had a barnyard. Boys had a point on going there many a time to get eggs, so they could play with them pretty girls, 'cause they couldn't court 'em. So now, a disease got into the chickens, the chickens all died out and they didn't have no eggs left, so when the old man catch those boys out there, he'd whip 'em cause he knowed they wasn't there for eggs. They were lyin'. And so, that's the way it go."

DOUG: "Old Lady from Brewster's not a circle. It's a straight line. See the person that's out first. He's standing out in front of these with his back to them. You know, like in slavery time they would play out in the audience, like they're facing the people. One person be out there, and he act out as they be singing the song.

'There's an old lady from Brewster'	He be dancing, doing some kind of dance, some kind of movement.
'Had two hens'	Hold up two fingers.
'and a rooster.'	Hold up one.
'The rooster died,'	Cross your hands over your chest.
'the old hen cried,'	Put your hands over your face,
'I can't lay eggs like I used to.'	Shake your head.
'Oh, Ma, you look, so.'	[Bessie — "That mean when they come in they looking for them."] When the Mother and Father come back home they looking for tracks of boys. You put one hand up over your eyes and look around.
'Oh, Pa, you look so.'	Put your other hand up over your eyes and look around. See, the girls would have to tell the truth. They wouldn't tell a lie. Then they would ask them:
'Who been here since I been gone?'	They seen the tracks. Well, they say:
'Two little boys with the red cap on.'	Hold up two fingers and tap your head with those fingers.
'Hang them boys on a hickory stick.'	
'Papa gonna parch them soon.	That's when all the pain will start!
'Pain in the head, etc.'	

MARY JO: "And when you do that you hold your head and jump for joy?" [By this I mean the step described by Ms. Hawes on page 44 of *Step It Down*.]

BESSIE: "Any kind of movement, just ring it, that's all!" (Great laughter.) "Just ring it! You get a whipping there, you hear? How would you feel, you getting a whipping!"

DOUG: "You don't stand still when you get a whipping!"

BESSIE: "I told a boy, laying there, now you got to *do* something, you got to wiggle yourself! He said, 'Wiggle?' He said, 'Say no more.' And that boy wiggled so, 'til I'm telling you, that whole house, it about rocked, that was the wiggliest, I never seen a man so lovely in my life. Some of them can really do it!"

Another fine call and response type selection, "Bob-a-needle" is also from *Step It Down*.

This singing game is very easy to learn and fun to play. The "Pawns" which follow the game are very interesting, particularly *"Wade in the Green Valley"*. Somehow this simple game brings back recollections of forfeits demanded in hosts of old tales.

It's a game. Of course, it's a play, too, but it's a game, a house game. . . . Or either you can play it outdoors.

"Bob-a-Needle" (bobbin needle?) is, for purposes of this game, a pen, a jackknife, or a small stick of wood that can be passed rapidly from hand to hand. All the players but one stand in a tight circle, shoulder to shoulder, holding their hands behind their backs. The extra player stands in the center of the ring; she closes her eyes and holds the bob-a-needle high over her head in one hand. One of the ring players silently creeps up and takes the bob-a-needle from her hand and puts it behind his own back. The center player then opens her eyes and begins singing the lead line of the song; the players in the circle sing the refrain:

LEAD VOICE (AD LIB)	GROUP VOICE
Bob-a-needle,	
	Bob-a-needle is a-running,
Bob-a-needle,	
	Bob-a-needle is a-running,
Better run, bob-a-needle,	
	Bob-a-needle is a-running,
Better hustle, bob-a-needle,	

I want bob-a-needle,

Want to find bob-a-needle,

Going to catch bob-a-needle,

Turn around, bob-a-needle,

Oh bob, bob-a-needle,

Bob-a-needle is a-running,

Bob-a-needle is a-running,

Bob-a-needle is a-running,

Bob-a-needle is a-running,

Bob-a-needle is a-running,

Bob-a-needle is a-running.

The lead singer's lines are extemporaneous and can be sung in any order. Mrs. Jones often sang each one twice.

During the singing, the players in the ring pass the bob-a-needle from hand to hand, trying to move as little as possible in order not to make its location obvious. Bob-a-needle may travel clockwise or counterclockwise, and the players may reverse direction at will. The center player meanwhile reaches around the waist and feels the hands of each ring player in turn; she too may go in either direction but she may not skip players nor run back and forth across the ring. When the center player reverses the direction of *her* search, she must signal this with the lead line, "Turn around, bob-a-needle!"

This game does not end when someone is caught holding the elusive bob-a-needle. Like most of Mrs. Jones's games that involve "losing," the person caught simply pays a forfeit and/or takes over the center role so that the play can begin again. When the players tire, the accumulated forfeits are redeemed by their owners in a new sequence of play.

Bob-a-Needle

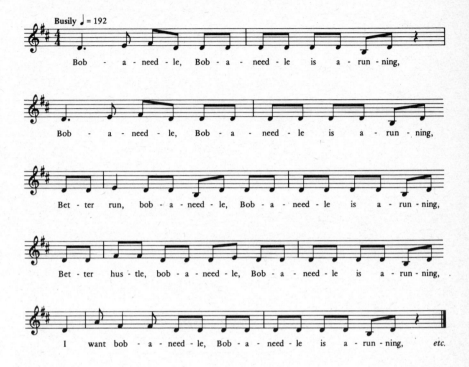

Bob - a - need - le, Bob - a - need - le is a - run - ning,

Bob - a - need - le, Bob - a - need - le is a - run - ning,

Bet - ter run, bob - a - need - le, Bob - a - need - le is a - run - ning,

Bet - ter hus - tle, bob - a - need - le, Bob - a - need - le is a - run - ning,

I want bob - a - need - le, Bob - a - need - le is a - run - ning, *etc.*

Pawns

In such games as "Bob-a-Needle" a player who "loses" does not leave the game, but gives up an article of clothing or some object in his possession to a selected referee, and the play goes on. When the players tire of the first game, the earning back of the "pawns" (the articles given up) forms a kind of coda — a relaxing end play to the game itself. (The Islanders used the term "pawn" for both the forfeited article and the task assigned to redeem it.)

To win back a pawn, a judge and a caller are necessary. The judge sits in a chair; the caller stands behind him and holds a pawned object over his head. The judge should not know what, or whose, the article is.

CALLER: Heavy, heavy, hangs over your head.

JUDGE: Is it ladies' wear or gentlemen's wear?

CALLER: It's [ladies'] wear. What shall be done to the [lady] that owns this wear?

The judge then orders the player in question to perform some action. Some of the "pawns" Mrs. Jones exacted were:

to bark like a dog
to crow like a rooster
to hop like a frog
to say a speech
to sing a song
to wade the green valley (see next play)

Mabel Hillary, of a later generation and "raised up with boys," required more vigorous and difficult pawns:

to stand on your head
to walk on your hands from there to me
to walk like a crab (The player lies down on his back, puts his hands on the floor by his shoulders and pushes up so that his body is held up by his feet and hands. He then "walks," spanking himself on the hips with his hands alternately.)
to walk like a duck (Player squats down, puts his arms around and then between his legs and holds his ankles while "walking.")
to roll the pumpkin (Player sits doubled up with arms wrapped around his knees, holding his ankles tightly with his hands, and rolls all the way over.)

Wade in the Green Valley

The one who is wading the green valley don't say a word; he answers by his feet. . . .

This play is actually a "pawn," a task set a player who wants to win back a forfeited article. The judge may tell him to call out a lady of his choice and "wade the green valley with her."

The gentleman then stands on one side of the room with his lady facing him on the other side. He asks her, "Do you like _____?"

(some kind of food, or a person, or a color, or anything he thinks of.) If she likes it, she takes one step forward; if she does not like it, she takes one step back. If she is indifferent or undecided, she stands still.

Mrs. Jones continues,

Now when you get close, he says, "Would you like a sweet kiss?" and you got to get that, so that's the last of it. Sometimes they take great big steps, if they like what he calls a lot. . . .

This can be played without being a pawn, Mrs. Jones tells me.

Just line your line of children up and let them wade the green valley — just see what would they say with their feet!

In play, this is extraordinarily dramatic; without music or rhythmic accompaniment, the human body makes its statement.

Among the most magical of the drama games for me are the winding games. Perhaps the Apple Tree, which follows is the best of them all. Both of these activities are taken from folklorist Richard Chase's *Singing Games and Playparty Games* (Dover).

I consider myself fortunate to have played the games discussed so far in this book with both Bessie Jones and Richard Chase. Since that time I have had great fun sharing them with children and adults. Improvising from these pieces with other verses and stories becomes a relatively easy matter.

Wind Up the Apple Tree

A large number of players can be accommodated in this game. The players join hands and form a loose spiral. A player at one end of the spiral is designated Winder. The player at the opposite end is the tree. The Players sing in march tempo:

PLAYERS:
Wind up the apple tree!
Hold on tight!
Wind it all day and
wind it all night!

The winder leads around clockwise while the tree stands still. As soon as any players' arm are stretched out he stops. One by one the players stop and so does the winder.

Stir up the dumplings,
the pot boils over!
Stir up the dumplings,
the pot boils over!

Winder and players terminate the winding up song and sing the jump song. Everyone jumps up and down on both feet as they sing. As this chorus is repeated again and again, the winder begins to sidestep to the left. The winder eventually pulls the spiral out straight.

Wind up the apple tree

Hold tight! etc.

WIND UP THE APPLE TREE

Steady march tempo. Sing it over and over until all are wound up.

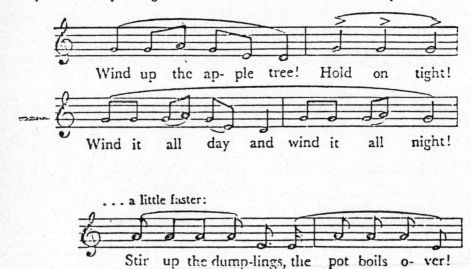

Wind up the ap- ple tree! Hold on tight!

Wind it all day and wind it all night!

. . . a little faster:

Stir up the dump-lings, the pot boils o- ver!

Here is another version of a winding game.

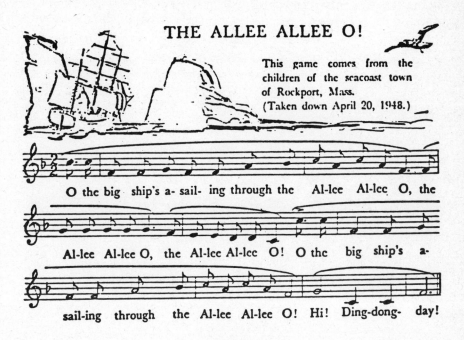

THE ALLEE ALLEE O!

This game comes from the children of the seacoast town of Rockport, Mass. (Taken down April 20, 1948.)

O the big ship's a- sail- ing through the Al-lee Al-lee O, the Al-lee Al-lee O, the Al-lee Al-lee O! O the big ship's a- sail-ing through the Al-lee Al-lee O! Hi! Ding-dong- day!

FORMATION

A line of players holding hands. The player on the left end of the line takes hold on a playground post, or leans with the left hand against a tree-trunk or a wall.

STEP

A quiet walk.

As the song begins, the one on the right-hand end of the line leads between the tree and the first player, thus winding up number one.

Then

the leader pulls around counter-clockwise and goes between number one and number two, winding up number two, etc. Each turns half-way around when wound up.

Keep on singing and keep on winding them up one by one . . .

. . . until the last one is wound up.

To unwind: Keep on singing, and . . .

the one next to the leader now lifts his left arm and pulls the leader back through.

Then the next pulls both these players through.

The next pulls these three through, etc., until all are unwound. To end, skip in a ring.

Johnny Cuckoo

With "Johnny Cuckoo," we leave the circle and the winding and return to the story told in a line. I like to set the scene before entering into this story.

"I want you to imagine that it is the middle of the night and you have been rousted from your beds by members of the home guard and herded into the village square. A major battle is in process along the front this night and reinforcements are required. A company commander has come to press you into service. As he approaches the villagers break into song. . . ."

Here comes one Johnny Cuckoo etc.

GROUP IN UNISON: Here comes one Johnny Cuckoo — single player walks
Cuckoo, Cuckoo toward the line of
Here comes one Johnny Cuckoo singers and marches
On a cold and stormy night. back and forth in-
specting the "soldier"

GROUP IN UNISON: What did you come for,
Come for, come for,
What did you come for
On a cold and stormy night?

PLAYER: I come for me (we come for us) — as Johnny Cuckoo
a soldier, delivers his message,
Soldier, soldier, players in the line
I come for me (we come for us) react in mime
a soldier
On a cold and stormy night.
(slight increase in tempo)

GROUP IN UNISON: You look too filthy dirty, — players all turn their
Dirty, dirty, backs on Johnny Cuckoo
You look too filthy dirty and wiggle their hips
On a cold and stormy night. at him, turning to
face him on the last
word

PLAYER: I am (we are) just as clean
as you are,
You are, you are,
I am (we are) just as clean
as you are,
On a cold and stormy night.

— Johnny Cuckoo turns
his back on the line
and wiggles his hips,
turning around and
choosing another
player on the last word

GROUP IN UNISON: Now here comes two Johnny
Cuckoos etc.

— game is repeated with
two Johnny Cuckoos, at
the end of which the
original Johnny
Cuckoo chooses another
player to repeat the
game with three and
so on.

Johnny Cuckoo

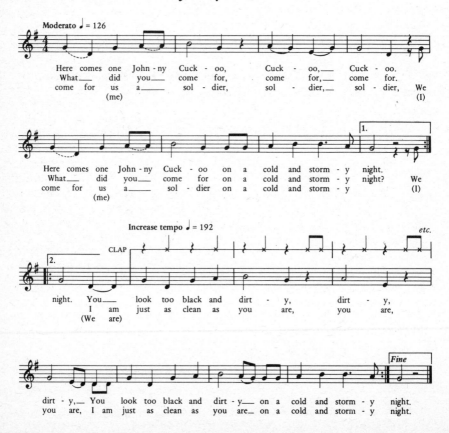

Moderato ♩ = 126

Here comes one John - ny Cuck - oo, Cuck - oo, Cuck - oo.
What___ did you___ come for, come for,___ come for.
come for us a___ sol - dier, sol - dier,___ sol - dier, We
(me) (I)

Here comes one John - ny Cuck - oo on a cold and storm - y night.
What___ did you___ come for on a cold and storm - y night?
come for us a___ sol - dier on a cold and storm - y We
(me) (I)

Increase tempo ♩ = 192   etc.

CLAP

2.
night. You___ look too black and dirt - y, dirt - y,
I am just as clean as you are, you are,
(We are)

Fine
dirt - y,___ You look too black and dirt - y___ on a cold and storm - y night.
you are, I am just as clean as you are___ on a cold and storm - y night.

I think that "Threadneedle," described beautifully by Bessie Jones in *Step It Down*, is the most intricate of all the drama games. Lines, arches, winding solos and group responses are all part of this miniature musical drama. All this by way of pointing out that in life people sometimes borrow things from us and fail to return them.

Players are lined up roughly by height from tallest to shortest, hands joined. Where there are more than a dozen players try two lines, spaced wide apart, playing simultaneously.

Threadneedle

TALLEST PLAYER A:	Neighbor, neighbor, lend me your hatchet.	— leans out of line and calls to other end
SHORTEST PLAYER 2:	Neighbor, neighbor, step up and get it.	— leans out of line and calls to head of the line

LEAD VOICE: OR PLAYER A	Nana	A starts walking and leads through the arch made by players B and C. B must turn under her own arm, (players do not hold hands tightly but allow the turners to rotate naturally and return to original position without a twisted wrist.) Player A continues leading the marching line around and through the arch between players C and D and so on. When the space between 1 & 2 has been sewn, the line returns to its original form.
GROUP:	threadneedle	
LEAD VOICE:	Nana	
GROUP:	threadneedle	
LEAD VOICE:	I wants my needle	
GROUP:	threadneedle	
LEAD VOICE:	My gold-eyed needle	
GROUP:	threadneedle	
LEAD VOICE:	My mama's needle	
GROUP:	threadneedle	
LEAD VOICE:	It's my only needle	
GROUP:	threadneedle	

PLAYER A:	Neighbor, neighbor, send me my hatchet.	Another conversation ensues as before
PLAYER 2:	Neighbor, neighbor I ain't got it!	
GROUP:	Going to wind up-a this bunkum, bunkum, Wind up-a this bunkum. Wind up-a this bunkum, bunkum, Wind up-a this bunkum.	2 skips out, leading the line. A stands still and the line is wound around A.
GROUP:	Going to shake down-a this bunkum, bunkum. Shake down-a this bunkum, bunkum Shake down-a this bunkum. Shake down-a this bunkum.	Hands still joined the spiral jumps up and down together singing
GROUP:	Going to unwind-a this bunkum, bunkum, Unwind-a this bunkum. Unwind-a this bunkum, bunkum, Unwind-a this bunkum. . . .	2 turns back, retraces her steps and brings the line back to the starting position.

Nana, Thread Needle

New words and new music adaptation by Bessie Jones; collected and edited by Alan Lomax. TRO—©
copyright 1972 Ludlow Music, Inc., New York, N.Y. Used by permission.

There are many short poems, verses and nursery rhymes that can easily become incorporated into the play circle. Here is a well-known Shel Silverstein piece played out as a little group drama.

THE SLITHEREE-DEE
The Slitheree-dee has crawled out of the sea.
He may catch all the others, but he won't catch me.
No you won't catch me, old Slitheree-dee,
You may catch all the others, but you wo------

Shel Silverstein

Players hold hands in a circle. Four other players take their place in the center of the big circle, link arms around waists, snort, stomp and generally make the Slitheree-dee as awesome as can be. Players crowd around the beast, as close as possible, hands linked and held high. They begin to chant the verse as they slowly retreat. When the circle has stretched back as far as possible, the players advance on the slitheree-dee, still chanting. As some point, the slitheree-dee separates and gives chase until a player is caught. The new and bigger slitheree-dee forms up and begins to snort and stomp. The remaining players reform the circle around the beast, close in then retreat slowly, chanting. The game continues until a giant slitheree-dee remains and the circle can no longer be formed around it.

My favorite nursery rhyme has always been *How Many Miles to Babylon.* I like to say the words and think about the implications of the journey made at night. In drama classes we have built lengthy improvisations out of it and enjoyed reading some of the books that this verse has inspired. I had used this rhyme for many years before I discovered that it could also be played as a drama game. Here are the instructions for playing it.

Two of the players join hands, and stand face-to-face, with their hands in front as if forming a gate. Each of these has a secret name. The other players form themselves into a line by clasping each other round the waist from behind. They go up to the two that form the gate, and the leader asks the first question. The dialogue then proceeds to the end.

How many miles to Babylon?
Three score and ten.
Can I get there o' candle-light?
There and back again.
Here's my black (raising one foot),
And here's my blue (raising the other),
Open the gates and let me through.

The two then lift their arms as high as they can, still joined, and the line of players passes through. All at once the two bring their arms down on one and make him (or her) prisoner. The prisoner is asked in a whisper, so as not to disclose the secret name, which of the two is to be chosen. The one so captured takes his (or her) stand behind the one chosen. The same process is gone through till all the players are taken captive, and have stationed themselves behind the one or the other of the two forming the gate. The two sides then have a tug of war.

Acting and Pretending Games:

Closely related to the drama games but perhaps less active are what Iona and Peter Opie have described as acting and pretending games.

In acting games, there is a story, often accompanied by set actions each time the game is played. These games are very old and usually involve the taking on of roles which children have always reveled in. Many of these games are somewhat grisly and involve corpses, witches, scarey old men and incarcerated damsels.

MARY BROWN

1 Here we all stand round the ring.
  And now we shut poor Mary in.
  Rise up, rise up, poor Mary Brown.
  And see your mother go through the town.

  Mary: I will not stand upon my feet
  To see my mother go through the street.

2 Children: Rise up, rise up, poor Mary Brown.
  And see your father go through the town.

Mary: I will not stand upon my feet
To see my father go through the street.

3 *Children: Rise up, rise up, poor Mary Brown.*
And see your brother go through the town.

Mary: I will not stand upon my feet
To see my brother go through the street.

4 *Sister.*

5 *Cousins.*

6 *Uncles.*

7 *Aunts.*

8 *Beggars.*

9 *Children: Rise up, rise up, poor Mary Brown.*
And see your sweetheart go through the town.

Mary: I will get up upon my feet
To see my sweetheart go through the street.

(And makes a rush to break the ring that surrounds her.)

Traditional English

From Iona and Peter Opie's *Children's Games in Street and Playground* comes this next acting game. A fine story to tell before or after the game is "Tipingee" from *The Magic Orange Tree*, tales from Haiti collected by Diane Wolkstein (see p. 34, chapter two).

Old Man in the Well

Any number of players may join in this game but one must be the mother, one the old man and all the rest are the mother's children. The old man hides himself in a gloomy, mysterious place which is designated as the well. The following dialogue takes place:

CHILDREN TO MOTHER: Mother Mother may we
                     have some bread and
                     butter?

MOTHER TO CHILDREN:	Let me see your hands. Your hands are very dirty. Go to the well and wash them.	(Children hold out their hands for inspection)
CHILDREN TO MOTHER:	Mother! Mother! There's an old man in the well!	(The children go to the well where they spy the old man hiding. They rush back to Mother screaming.)
MOTHER TO CHILDREN:	Don't be silly children. There's no one in the well.	
CHILDREN TO MOTHER:	But we saw him!	
MOTHER TO CHILDREN:	It's only your father's underwear. I hung them out to dry. Go again.	
CHILDREN TO MOTHER:	Mother! Mother! There's an old man in the well!	(The children go again, see the old man and come back screaming.)

The mother tells them again that no one is in the well and makes up another explanation such as it's only your father's shirt hanging out to dry.

The children are sent back two or three more times until the mother is persuaded to come too. She sends one of the children for a candle (twig) lights it and accompanies the children to the well.

When they reach the well, she is about to look in, the old man blows the candle out.

MOTHER TO NEAREST CHILD:	Why did you blow out my candle?	(She pretends to cuff the child about. Child sets up a howl)

The mother relights the candle. The old man blows it out.

MOTHER TO ANOTHER CHILD:	Why did you blow out my candle?	(A second child is beaten in a mock fight and howls lustily)

119

This action is repeated until every child has had an opportunity for a dramatic howl.

Finally, the old man permits the mother to look into the well. He leaps out screaming and gives chase. The person caught becomes the next old man.

Pretending games deal more with real activities and call for more improvisation. Usually they are less lurid than acting games. In these games, the players adopt a role within some common situation that they all understand and appreciate. "Lemonade" is a fine example of a pretending game.

Lemonade

The players divide into two equal teams and stand on parallel goals twenty or more feet apart. The first team decides on a trade or occupation to be acted out, and then advances toward the other team while the following dialogue takes place.

First team: Here we come.
Second team: Where from?
First team: New York.
Second team: What's your trade?
First team: Lemonade.
Second team: Give us some.

The first team comes as near to the second as they dare and acts out their trade or occupation each in his own way. The second team tries to identify what is being acted out, and when one identifies correctly the first team runs for its goal, while the second team tries to tag them. All who are tagged join the taggers' side. Second team chooses a trade and the dialogue is repeated, followed by the acting, as before. Both sides have the same number of turns, and the one having the largest number of players at the end wins.

Whenever these rhymes, games, stories and songs are played, I am always amazed to see how quickly self-consciousness drops away and is replaced by lively expressions and animated faces. This is very rewarding for it serves to illustrate that our interest and love of the material helps us to bring energy to the event.

Even more rewarding is the flood of memories that are released as fragments of verse, expressions, rhymes and stories come to mind and are spoken. People are often surprised at the extent of their own folk heritage. They are even more surprised that they had never thought to make use of it. How odd it is that we so often forget that which we have carried around inside of us all our lives!

Close Reading:

Close reading involves a host of activities, which encourages readers or listeners to pay attention to their own personal responses and to discover layers of meaning.

How words should be spoken; the intent of the storyteller; imagined contexts for the words; the exploration of secrets both inside and outside the story constitute some possible approaches.

Michael Rosen's poem "JoJo" from *You Can't Catch Me* might be explored as follows:

JOJO

I am Jojo
give me the sun to eat.
I am JoJo
give me the moon to suck.

The waters of my mouth
will put out the fires of the sun:
the waters of my mouth
will melt the light of the moon.

Day becomes night,
night becomes day.
I am JoJo
listen to what I say.

The children read the poem in unison. Then they divide the selection into two parts and read it antiphonally (the windshield wiper again). For example:

Group A: I am JoJo, give me the sun to eat.

Group B: I am JoJo, give me the moon to suck.

Next have the children work with different emotional states as they read.

Group A: powerful and determined

Group B: uncertain, hesitant

After one or two practice tries the children can pair-off and invent their own emotional states.

Now try different physical states. For example, person A has a cold nose in the nose.

Person B is at the bottom of a well.

By now, the children should be starting to view the selection in terms of its possibilities. Encourage the children to adopt roles and re-read the selection with a partner or divide the class in half.

You and the children might need to make a list of possible roles. For example, a giant and the sea; a mountain top and the wind; the Greek god Zeus and a boastful rival; a demon and a sea monster; a robot and thunder.

Once the children have explored possible roles, have them form groups of four and select one voice to act out loud. Before working with the voice, the children must try to imagine why the words are being spoken and who is being addressed.

Many of the children will probably want to add body movement to accompany the words. Encourage it.

When the children have worked out their interpretation, have them reassemble in the story circle. Each group, in turn, can now tell the story.

An example of some of the stories I have witnessed is: A group of girls sit on the floor, arms linked, swaying powerfully back and forth, together, rhythmically, making with vocal sounds the toss of waves upon a beach. Then each, in turn, chants two lines. Then the group chants the last four. The swaying subsides and ceases. "You're the sea!" cry their classmates.

"Yes, but who are we talking to?"

"The beach, the shore, land."

"Right! Why?"

There is silence; one girl explains, "We were thinking that the land and the sea were having a contest to prove who was stronger . . . something like when the sun and the wind tried to get a man to remove his cloak in a story I once read."

I have also witnessed the voice of a giant baby who gives his mother considerable difficulty, the voice of an alien who has come to claim the earth and the voice of a child, who is bullied frequently at school, stomping around his room and glaring into a mirror.

In each case, the children have stimulated their listeners with a lively interpretation of the poem. They have understood the potential of a story for a range of interpretations.

A group of teachers made of this story a tribal event accompanied by the powerful rhythms of drums as the shaman warned the tribe about an impending eclipse of the sun.

Always at the conclusion of all these tellings, we examine the collection from which the poem is taken. Quentin Blake has illustrated this poem quite wonderfully. In the lower left corner of the double page spread, a child stands in his bed holding an orange in one hand ("give me the sun to eat") and a crescent-shaped cookie in the other ("give me the moon to suck"). From the mountains of the bed sheets and blankets, a giant, completely filling the entire right hand side of the spread, cradles the moon in one hand and reaches out to grab the sun.

The children can all appreciate Blake's brilliant visual depiction, while basking in the glow of their own equally exciting oral interpretations.

Try similar explorations with:

PUDDEN TAME

What's your name?
Pudden Tame.
What's your other?
Bread and Butter.
Where do you live?
In a sieve
What's your number?
Cucumber.

Traditional

MOONWUZO'S SEA SONG

Who is that walking on the dark sea sand?
The old Bride of the wind.
Who is that staring out of the weedy pool?
The newborn monster in its caul!
What is that eerie chanting from the foam?
The mermaid's gardening song.
What is that shadow floating on the water?
The Fish King's daughter.
Who bears those candles down by the curled rim?
The children going home.

Cara Lockhart Smith

1. Cut the poem into strips of one line each.

Mix them up and make enough complete sets so that five or six groups each have one set.

2. Have the children arrange the strips into what they think the story should be.

3. Have each group prepare to read their version in the form of a ritual. Encourage movement, dance, sound effects with the reading.

4. Once the readings have been shared, examine the original poem. Perhaps the whole group could now read antiphonally. Vary the parts and read again.

5. Ask the children what creatures are familiar to them. Which are unfamiliar? What do all these creatures have in common?

6. Brainstorm a list of supernatural water creatures. For example, nymphs, sirens, tritons, selchies and so on.

7. Have the children move into small groups. Each group is to claim one sea creature from the list and feature it in a group tableau. Each tableau should have one moveable part that operates in slow motion.

8. Now in call and response fashion, tell the story together. The whole group will pose the question "Who is that?" and so on, and in turn each small group will chant what they are from the tableau story.

Inside and outside a story are many secrets that can be discovered. Searching for these secrets, finding these other stories, imagining the storytellers who could be telling them, help build understanding of the story and reveal its relationships to other stories. Word-by-word, line-by-line examination can lead to the following exploration of:

There was a maid on Scrabble Hill
And if not dead, she lives there still.
She grew so tall, she touched the sky
And on the moon, hung clothes to dry.

* Chant to skipping rope rhythms in unison, orchestrate chorally, employing many solo voices and group parts or sing it to familiar tunes.
* Invent ritual movement to accompany the words. Many stories from the oral tradition were accompanied by actions or movement sequences. In some instances, a story's passage through time has

resulted in either the loss of movement pattern or the loss of story details. Could it be that *The Scrabble Hill Maid* once had a pattern of movement to accompany the words?

* Imagine who might have told the story "There was a maid on Scrabble Hill" and recreate that voice aloud.
* List as many possible speakers for the words as possible. Brainstorming becomes very important in order to produce many ideas. Once there is a good range of possibilities narrow the choices down to those which seem to lie within the framework of the story. When a choice has been made, work on the voice out loud using unison or multi-part techniques. Gather everyone together and retell the story. The range of possible contexts which have been imposed on the four lines will be quite remarkable. In the course of one session I have heard the lines spoken by:

— a tour guide describing a rock formation used by local residents as a sign post to a mountain pass.
— a side show carney urging us to step behind the canvas to view the tall geeky lady inside.
— the voices of children playing a chasing game in the manner of "What time is it Mr. Wolf?"
— grandparents relating a ghost story to wide-eyed grandchildren
— old folks on a porch reminiscing about childhood experiences
— spies sending a code message behind enemy lines
— the celestial voice of the dreamweaver creating a spell
— the sepulchral voice of the maid herself, returned from the dead to haunt the hill

Explore questions that the story raises. Most groups have little difficulty filling a page. Here is a random sample of the kinds of questions often posed about "The Maid".

— Were her extreme differences (her size and nocturnal behavior) a cause for personal distress or personal triumph?
— Was she the village washerwoman? Did she really hang clothes on the moon? How do you hang clothes on the moon? Could she do it only when there was a crescent moon? Were the phases of the moon actually accomplished by the woman in order to satisfy her drying needs?
— Is this a verse used to describe a pattern of stars near the moon?
— Why was the hill called Scrabble Hill?
— Who might live on a hill with that name? Who left the hill and

why? Do folks live there yet? Is there a Scrabble Hill in your community?

— Is this the maid herself talking? Did things ever change for her? Is this her recollection of what others said about her? Is this her form of self-parody? What makes some people the subject of taunting and torment?

Conduct interviews in role. For example, set this scene for the children:

"You all grew up on Scrabble Hill. Many years ago you left, but today you have returned to visit the place you once knew so well. In a few moments you will return to view familiar sights. As you wander about the hill, survey as many people as you can. Ask them if they remember the 'Scrabble Hill Maid'. Ask them if they know any stories about her."

At the end of the activity, ask everyone to sit down and rewrite the nursery rhyme retaining only the original opening line and revealing in the remaining three lines what each understands about the story now they have heard so many tales.

Form a story circle and tell the new stories. Through these simple rhymes, hypotheses about that little story are shared, imagined voices are added to the story and I am certain that the group now understands something of the exciting process of building and discovery which storytelling involves.

Here are some new tales that have emerged:

There was a maid on Scrabble Hill
Who frightened every Jack and Jill
Were we so very, very small
That we all thought her 'extra-tall'?

There was a maid on Scrabble Hill
Who choked upon her iron pill
Her neck grew stiff; it would not bend
Her stiff-necked stance caused lots of friends.

There was a maid on Scrabble Hill
She loved to sit beside her still
*She drank and drank from her big cup**
And now she cannot give it up.

* the cup referred to is supposed to be the Big Dipper.

There was a maid on Scrabble Hill
Who stared at folk and gave them chills
She slept all day and walked the night
And gave us all a terrible fright.

There was a maid on Scrabble Hill
Her love has gone — she waits there still
She hangs out beacons — higher, higher
To lead him home — her heart's desire.

Between and beyond the lines of such little stories as *The Scrabble Hill Maid*, are dozens of stories if we just take the time to think of them. Indeed some of the most poignant storytelling by children, I have heard, has emerged from our attempts to create a set of stories around such little tales.

"Saturday Night" is another wonderful tale to explore:

On Saturday night I lost my wife,
And where do you think I found her?
Up in the moon singing a tune,
With all the stars around her.

Among the stories, inside the story, which children have been quick to identify are:

(a) attempts to return the woman to earth;
(b) the circumstances that led to the woman's journey into the skies;
(c) woman's concerns about adapting to a new environment;
(d) why the singing was so important to the adventure.

For each of these stories, the children attempted to identify the storytellers. For example, in the story of attempts to return the woman to earth, some children decided that the villagers were telling the story. They figured that music was important in the situation and they decided to try and "sing the woman down". Sound poems were created using imaginary moon words and chanted after considerable experimentation with the sound possibilities of the words. When all the poems had been chanted, the villagers were asked to reflect on the event as they recalled it years later and to report what the results had been.

On another occasion, the storytellers were relatives of the woman and the woman herself. In this instance relatives paired off with the woman and attempted to persuade her to return home.

Relatives tried to convince the woman that there were many earthly pleasures that she would eventually miss. Those role playing the woman countered with fantastical descriptions of the new life in space.

An examination of other folktales detailing similar situations evolved from these speculations on the story. Among them, Alden Nowlan's splendid retelling of the Micmac legend *The Star Brides*.

THE STAR BRIDES

In the days of the people who are gone, two beautiful young sisters were overtaken by night in the woods.

Knowing they could not hope to return to their village before daylight, they made themselves beds of pine boughs and lay down under the open sky, huddling together for warmth.

As they waited for the coming of sleep, they talked, as young girls will, of the young men they might one day marry.

The sky was cloudless and the stars were very bright. Sleep was slow in coming and the sisters were a little afraid. To comfort one another, they pretended the stars were the eyes of lovers, looking down at them protectively.

"I will choose that one to be my husband," said the elder sister, pointing at the sky. "His eyes are as bright as those of a hawk."

"And I will choose that one," said the younger sister, gesturing drowsily, "his eyes are as bright as those of an eagle."

The sisters laughed, fell silent and drifted off to sleep.

Then it was morning. Even before opening her eyes, the elder sister stretched her beautiful arms and legs.

"Be careful!" cried a voice, "you will spill my warpaint!"

Suddenly, the sisters were fully awake. They sat up quickly, their eyes wide with wonderment.

Here were two handsome young warriors. One, with eyes like those of a hawk, leaned on his spear. The other, with eyes like those of an eagle, knelt on the ground to mix his red warpaint.

Perhaps it was in that first instant of awakening that the sisters fell in love. Perhaps it took many days. Perhaps they only imagined that they were in love. In any event, it was not long before they were married: the elder sister to the warrior with the eyes of a hawk; the younger to the warrior with the eyes of an eagle.

For a time, they were happy. While their husbands hunted in the woods, the sisters cared for their wigwams.

But soon the sisters grew sulky because, near the wigwams, there was a large, flat stone which their husbands had strictly forbidden them to touch or move.

If their interest had not been aroused by their husbands' prohibition, the sisters might never have thought of touching the stone. As it was, they could not rest until their curiosity was satisfied.

So one day when the men were hunting for bear, the sisters pried up the stone and peered under it.

What they saw made them start back and cry out with fear. For the stone was like a trapdoor in the roof of the world.

Far, far below they saw the village of their childhood, surrounded by the forest in which they had fallen asleep.

"Our husbands are not men!" cried the elder sister.

"They are wizards!" cried the younger.

"They are star creatures!"

"And they have taken us to their home above the sky!"

The sisters embraced one another and wept and when their husbands returned home they would not leave off weeping.

"Did you not choose us to be your husbands?" the hawk-eyed man demanded.

"Did you not summon us when you lay in the forest?" demanded the eagle-eyed man.

"That was only a game," wept the elder sister.

"All girls play such games," wept the younger.

"Then you wish to return to your world?" asked the hawk-eyed man.

"Yes. Oh, yes. Please," the sisters agreed.

"Then you are free to go," said the man with the eyes of an eagle. "But you must follow our instructions."

That night the sisters were told they must sleep together, and they were to cover their faces.

"In the morning you must not be in haste to uncover your

faces," the star men warned. "Wait until you hear a chickadee sing; and even then you must not open your eyes. Wait still longer until you hear the red squirrel sing; and still you must wait. Keep your faces covered and your eyes closed until you hear the striped squirrel sing. Then open your eyes and uncover your faces and you will be safe."

The sisters sleep little that night and awoke early the following morning. They lay awake for a long time with their faces covered before they heard the singing of the chickadee.

The younger sister wanted to get up at once to see if they had in truth been returned to earth, but the elder sister restrained her.

"We must wait until the singing of the striped squirrel," she reminded. "Be patient. We will soon be back in our own village."

But when the red squirrel sang, the younger sister could control herself no longer. She uncovered her face and opened her eyes. And the moment she opened her eyes she found herself falling through the night — falling faster and faster toward the stony floor of the world.

There was not even time for her to cry out, so her sister did not know she had disappeared until she heard the singing of the striped squirrel, uncovered her face, opened her eyes and found herself in the part of the forest where their adventures had begun.

However, as she looked up at the sky from which she had lately come, the elder sister saw a star falling through the gray of the early morning and knew that star was in fact her younger sister who had uncovered her eyes too soon and was doomed to fall forever toward the earth.

And to this very day when the people see a falling star they say it is the younger sister, still tumbling through the night.

There are even those who say that the morning star is the hole in the sky through which the eagle-eyed warrior observes the eternal descent of his bride.

Here is another nursery rhyme chock-a-block with possibilities for storying.

> There are men in the village of Erith
> Whom nobody seeth or heareth
> And there looms on the marge
> Of the river, a barge
> That nobody roweth or steereth

Louise Cullen, a program consultant with the North York Board of Education wrote the haunting tune which follows. Sing it together then try the piece as a two-part round.

Work with the sounds of dripping oars and add movements. Perhaps the children could build imaginary barges and row in time to the round. Quite a bit of build-up could be tried here.

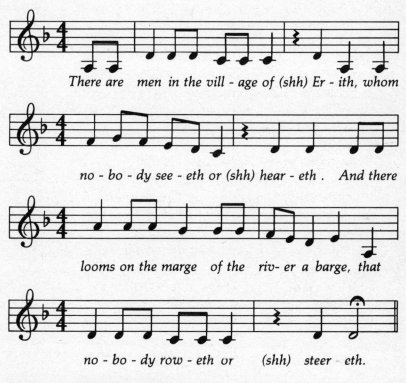

There are   men in the vill - age of (shh) Er - ith, whom

no - bo - dy see - eth or (shh) hear - eth .   And there

looms on the marge   of the   riv- er a barge, that

no - bo - dy row - eth or   (shh)   steer - eth.

• Music — Louise Cullen © 1983
• Lyrics — P.D. — The Annotated Mother Goose
      Gould & Gould, N.Y., The World Pub. Co., 1967

If you wish to proceed further, have the children invent a variety of contexts into which the words can be placed. (Who is the storyteller, why is the story being told and to whom.)

As a further step, explore the mystery of the barges. Possibly explore the dilemma these barges pose for the residents of Erith. Have the children role play the villagers. Explain to them:

> "Strange barges have tied up at your wharves. No living being has been seen coming from or going to the barges. They show no sign of leaving."

> "What concerns do you have about these barges?" (group idea finding)

> "Take your concerns to the mayor".
> "What messages must the mayor carry to the barges?"

After exploring the possibilities through role playing, tell the children:

> "Many years ago strange barges tied up at the wharves in the village of Erith. What stories are still told of that event? (Try to include the nursery rhyme in your tale.)

All stories, not just the little texts we have examined, have secrets to yield. Here is a fine tale by Richard Kennedy that will be considered in terms of its secrets.

THE LOST KINGDOM OF KARNICA

All things were not especially fine or wonderful in the Kingdom of Karnica before the stone was found, but the land was rich and yielding, and there was work and food for the people and a pleasant life for most. The king had never had the temptation to do anything really evil or the opportunity to do anything fatally foolish. And of course he had a wise man to give him good advice. But life got worse, and quickly, after the stone was found.

The story of how the stone was found was told many hundreds of times in those last days, and the manner of it was this: Farmer Erd was digging a well, a very deep well because of his ordinary bad luck, when he struck into the stone with his pick. He tried for half a day to dig around it, but with no luck, for the stone was enormous. Then he went home to sleep on the problem.

The next day he got neighbor Grum to come help him. They took torches and tools to the bottom of the well. Farmer Erd had the idea that they could split the stone with a chisel and take it out in pieces. Grum held the chisel and Erd hit it with a sledgehammer. "Whank! Whank! Whank!"

"Don't hit my muckle-muckle hand!" Grum cussed.

"I wouldn't hit your muckle-muckle hand," Erd said.

"Whank! Whank! Whank!"

A few chips jumped up from the stone, but it wouldn't split. Erd wiped his brow. "What kind of muckle-muckle stone is that?" he said.

"I'll be muckle-muckle if I know," said Grum.

"Let's give it a look," said Erd, taking up his flask of water. He poured some water on the stone and rubbed at it with his shirt-tail. Soon they could see in the fluttering torchlight that they were kneeling on a smooth red stone. Rainbows of light shone from it and washed like surf across the surface and settled back in golden-red pools of internal fire. It was obvious even to Erd and Grum that this was a precious stone, and it was bigger than a horse.

The men gasped and breathed out in awe and reverence, "Muckle-muckle!"

Erd and Grum then took an oath and swore on their mothers' graves to keep this find a secret, and they chipped off from the stone what they figured would be about a thousand dollars worth of precious gem stones.

That evening Farmer Erd had a dinner and a party for every relative of his he could find, and there were fifty-three of them at dinner, and more showed up later. Neighbor Grum went to town and bought drinks several times in several public places, and both men paid their costs with the flickering red gems.

Everyone knew about the stone in the well by ten o'clock in the next morning. And so did the king.

"I'll have a look at that," said the king. He was taken to the place upon his royal litter. He looked into the well, and his royal goldsmith and royal jeweler went down into the hole to make a close inspection. They came out of the hole with the report that the stone was precious and of the highest quality. The king told Erd and Grum that some king's men would assist in digging up the stone. He was lifted up in his litter, and he called out as the royal party left the place, "Dig it up! Jump to it!" And they jumped to it and began to dig up the stone right away.

The king's men worked all through the day while the news of the stone traveled around the kingdom. By dusk a thousand people had gathered to watch the working men who climbed in and out of the hole carrying dirt and water and tools. Washers and polishers were sent into the hole to make it shine like a jewel as it was being dug clear of the earth. The hole grew larger and a mound of dirt surrounded it. But the workers could not come to the edge of the stone, and at the end of the day the hole was forty feet across. Erd and Grum strutted about, telling their story and giving instructions that no one paid any attention to.

The king ordered on a night shift. That night he stood at a palace window and looked out across the darkened fair fields of Karnica to the mellow glow of torches where the stone lay. "Rich," he muttered, "rich!" A minister at his elbow leaned forward and said in his ear, "Indeed, Sire. We shall be the richest kingdom in the world . . . or elsewhere."

All night the king's men worked, and the next morning the day shift came on. By midday the hole was so large that the king ordered all those who had come to watch to go to their homes and return with picks, shovels and wheelbarrows, and they also went into the hole to work. The king himself moved to the site to give his personal attention to the labor. A banquet table was set up, and the king nibbled on grapes and dainties while attendants flocked about for his comfort's sake. They could hear him mutter under the linen napkin he dabbed to his mouth, "Rich, rich!" Several times the king was lifted in his chair and the banquet table moved back to make room for the widening hole. The workers worked all that day and all that night.

On the third day of digging, Farmer Erd's barn and house and fences were torn down as the hole reached out like a whirlpool. And then Neighbor Grum's farm was taken under, and the others. A circular hill of earth and debris grew up all about the hole, and there was no end yet to the great stone.

The wise man of the kingdom had not been idle all this while. He had been thinking, and wondering, and he had been studying his books. For long hours he had stood on the edge of the hole and gazed into the depths of the stone, which seemed to him to burn with a living and moving fire. His thoughts went deep into this mystery, and at length he reached a conclusion.

Touching a knee before the king, and touching a hand to his breast, he said, "The stone is the heart of the kingdom."

The king paused between grapes, glanced at his minister, who smiled, and then the king said to the wise man, "Don't make me laugh."

In another day the royal treasury was half used up from hiring workers from neighboring kingdoms. The hole was now as big as sixty farms and four hundred fields, but there was no sign that the workers were coming to the edge of the stone. On the next day the royal treasury was completely used up, and the royal palace was torn down to make room for the hole. The people of the kingdom and the workers lived in tents around the edge of the hole, and torches and campfires blazed at night around the great circle like the rim of a volcano. Inside the royal tent the king could be heard muttering, "Rich, rich!"

The wise man, sitting in his tent with a few books and a candle, sent word to the king asking permission to see him again. He was received in the king's tent. The minister was rolling up a map, and looked at the wise man sidelong and suspiciously.

The wise man dropped to a knee before the king, "The stone is the heart of the kingdom," he said. "And if we remove it, the kingdom will die."

The minister grunted, and the king said, "That's just a lot of muckle-muckle. Go away."

That was exactly the wise man's intention. He went about that night to several encampments, and in the glowing blood-red light reflected from the stone he spoke his wisdom that it should be passed about as a warning to all. For his trouble, he received only scoffing and sarcasm. On the following day the wise man bundled his few belongings together and walked to the ocean shore. There he found a man with a boat who promised to keep his books dry, and they sailed to another land.

Lakes were emptied, forests were cut down and rivers were turned to spill over the stone and wash it. Many more workers were hired, and great machines were invented that could dig faster than men, and everything was paid for with pieces of the stone. The hooves of horses were tied about with layers of soft leather, and messengers galloped across the gleaming surface of the stone carrying instructions and messages. At night, the thudding rhythm of the horses galloping across the stone sounded like a heartbeat to those who lay quietly on the earth and who listened.

The dirt piled up all around the edge of the stone like a range of hills, and then the day came when the workers had reached the borders of the neighboring kingdoms, and yet the stone was solid in the earth. All the tents of the workers were crowded onto the ocean shore of the Kingdom of Karnica. The king could not dig into the other kingdom's lands, and besides, part of the stone would belong to them if he did so. He studied the situation carefully, and then gave his orders. "Yank it out! Yank the muckle-muckle thing out!"

But it is much easier to decide to yank a stone out of the ground than it is to yank it out. Because all the land of the kingdom was dug up, the workers would have to pull at the stone from the shore of the ocean, and from boats and ships out in the sea. Therefore, many hundreds of boats and ships were bought and built to do the work, and many fishermen and sailors and crabbers were hired to man the flotilla. More engineers were hired, and great winches were constructed on the beach to haul at the stone.

The plan was this: long ropes were attached to the boats and ships, and to the winches on the shore, and then fastened to the stone in many inventive ways. It was hoped that all the hundreds of boats and ships and winches would lift the great red stone out of the earth on the outgoing tide and wind.

When the sun was on the horizon, the wind and tide swept out with a mighty lust, and the great red stone lifted from the earth and rolled over everyone on the beach and disappeared into the deeps, taking with it to the bottom of the ocean every boat and ship. The waters of the ocean crashed into the empty hole and caused a storm which lasted for six days.

*Then it was quiet and still. And there now ebbs a dark sea
where the heart of the Kingdom of Karnica was torn from the
breast of the earth.*

*That is the end of the story. The place is gone, and the
people are gone. We shall not hear of them again. Surely it is
a muckle-muckle shame, but it is the muckle-muckle truth.*

I had been telling this story to a class of grade six children one
day and at the conclusion of the story, I showed them the book from
which I had learned the story.

When they saw that the story was illustrated they asked immediately to see the part where the waters of the ocean were displaced by
the falling stone. During the examination of the picture one girl
exclaimed, "It's not anything like what I saw in my mind. In my
imagination I thought about the sea creatures struggling to get out of
the turmoil, but I don't see any creatures in this picture."

As we turned the pages and looked at other illustrations we
talked about what the artist had chosen to illustrate and how we had
imagined those things to be. We all agreed that the pictures were
interesting, but that we had visualized many other things.

At this point I drew a circle on the chalkboard and asked the
children to help me find all the stories within the story that we might
suggest a reader think about in any further illustrations we might
draw. Here are some of the children's suggestions:

The story about
people giving up their
homes to make room
for the digging. How
this was accomplished
and how people felt.

The engineers who found ways
to fasten the ropes to the stone
escaped before the disaster. How
did they fasten the ropes? Did
they know it wasn't a safe plan?

Some people fled
the kingdom before the
disaster. How did they
plan? What did they take?
Did they do this in secret?

Workers made up work songs
to cheer them as they dug.
How they sang those songs early
in the story and how they
sang them later is a story.

The wiseman
failed to stop the
king because he was
not able to put up
strong enough arguments.
How the people helped
him build a better case
should be told.

The story about
how the children
managed to lead a normal
life in the upheaval. The
games and songs they
made up about the
gigantic hole being
dug in their kingdom.

The stories identified by the children were all potentially interesting. The opportunity was there to add our own words and
thoughts to the story.

These children were keen to work on strengthening the
wiseman's arguments, so the class was divided into groups of five. In
each group there was to be a wise person and four advisors. It was
the job of the advisors to furnish the wise person with strong

arguments that might deter the king from the foolish course he was following.

I played a very determined and ruthless king who met with many delegations led by their wise person. At times the debating grew quite heated and many of the children became very agitated. When I stopped the role playing, we sat down to discuss what had happened. In the discussion there was much questioning about freedom and authority and power and whether that kind of thing happened in the modern world. Before they knew it, the children were discussing current events and the concepts of dictatorship and democracy. When they left school that day, I was sure they could never encounter that story again without thinking about all the ideas, all the issues, that story yielded. Each time I tell that story, I am ever mindful of those discussions and how much they have helped me to bring out not only aspects of greed, but concern for the people caught up in the frenzy of events that plunged recklessly along out of control.

By surrounding *The Lost Kingdom of Karnica* with a set of stories exploring the story's secrets, these children had done exactly what any good illustrator would do to enrich and extend the story experience.

Try to find Fiona French's illustrated version of the old ballad *John Barleycorn* (Abelard-Schuman, 1982) then work with poet Geoffrey Summerfield's ballad "Washday Battle", which follows. Have the children invent a set of stories to surround it using sound exploration, singing, movement, choral speaking and readers' theatre. A sample set of activities is provided to help you get started. This method of developing the surrounding stories is known as ensemble drama.

WASHDAY BATTLE

On washday in the good old bad old days
Before the launderette, machine and drier,
My mother used to use her own bare hands,
A posher, mangle, line, a wooden horse and fire.

At dawn she blew small coals into a blaze
Under well-water in a brim-full copper,
Soon as the water seethed and steamed into a haze
The clothes were seized. They plunged, and came a cropper.

Submerged, they scalded, lunged and tossed,
Squelched by fire-water through and through,
Until she gripped her soggy wooden stick
And levered them, steaming, out, all black and blue.

Carried them, soggy and limply dripping,
Chucked them onto the washboard-tub,
Where she set to, and thumped and slapped
And poshed and punched them, rub-a-dub.

Then she grabbed each punch-drunk one in turn
Wrung its neck, squeezed all its juice outright.
Corkscrewed and throttled, flat out it lay, quite dead,
And then she set to again, and beat it white.

Straightway she fed it to the lion-roaring mangle,
Into tight-rolling rubber lips, which sucked it in
Then slurped it out again, pancaked
To a wafer, breathless, depressed, and thin.

And then she flung them over her arm,
Hauled them out to the windy backyard plot,
Shook them out, cracked them like a whip,
Then strung them up and hanged the lot.

Soon as the wind possessed those wretched shapes,
Their arms would wildly wave, their legs kick free,
The skirts would billow out, voluminous,
And all the washing blew out, flew out, on the spree.

Mimicking Nelson's flags (England expects . . .)
They semaphored 'A Terrible To-do!'
'Clothes Saved From Drowning.' 'All Hands Saved!'
'Housewife Fails Again To Drown This Gallant Crew!'

From *Welcome*
Geoffrey Summerfield

Any or all of the following activities might be used to elaborate
aspects of "Washday Battle." The most fun might be to develop some

of the activities in groups, then come to the story circle to add all the parts in order.

(a) Sound Composition

Using found instruments and vocal sound, create an overture for the ballad. Key words or phrases such as "posher", "mangle", "seethed", "steamed" or "squeezed" might form the framework for the composition.

(b) Folk Song

Using a familiar tune or one invented by the group, set the opening stanza to music.

A brief refrain using the line "a posher, mangle, line, a wooden horse and fire" could be used to permit listeners to chime in.

(c) Dance

Try to capture in dance or movement the experience of the laundry as it is "scalded, banged, tossed, squeezed, corkscrewed and throttled."

The revival sequence — "kick free, blew out, flew out" — could be done in semaphore fashion.

Traditional game patterns outlined earlier in this chapter might be used.

(d) Choral Dramatization

Prepare stanzas three, five, eight, and nine for choral dramatization.

Varied shading (loud soft, high low pitch), sound exploration, repetition, antiphonal choruses and solo voices could all be incorporated.

(e) Story Theater

Create tableaux for stanzas two, four and six.

Employ voice-over narration to handle the words while the tableaux depict the scenes.

Come to the story circle and put everything together.

From Byrd Baylor's *A God On Every Mountaintop* (Scribner) comes this little tale which has numerous opportunities for storying and storytelling.

FROM SANDIA MOUNTAIN TO SKY PUEBLO

Up on Sandia Mountain
Spider Woman has her home.

Once long ago a man
from Sandia Pueblo
climbed up there to ask
for Spider Woman's help.

He said his wife
had been stolen away
and taken to a pueblo in the sky
where he could never go.

Spider Woman spun a web
that reached from the mountain
straight up through the stars
to Sky Pueblo.
Hidden by darkness,
they traveled along
that gleaming spiderweb bridge.

The man found his wife
and they hurried back over the web
to the mountain
and down to their home
in the valley.

When Spider Woman pulled her web
out of the sky
there was no way for anyone up there
to guess how they had come . . . or gone.

(a) Round-robin storytelling

Form the class into groups of four. Have each group read the story silently.

When the story has been read, it is put aside.

Number off in each group. On a prearranged signal from the teacher, number one begins to tell the story in his or her own words. Each time the teacher signals, the next teller takes over. In this way, no one person is totally responsible for telling the whole story.

If the groups have successfully managed to tell the tale proceed to activity B. It is possible they might need to go through the story once more as a whole class.

(b) First person narrations

Have the groups brainstorm all the possible story characters who could tell the story. (They can be actual — Spider Woman, the kidnap victim, the husband; or invented — a sky god, a passing eagle and so on.)

Each group is to decide the one character through whose eyes the story will now be attempted, use the same round-robin approach.

(c) Multi-part narration

Have each group select one third person narrator who will be responsible for shaping and directing the story through narrative.

Have each of the other group members choose a different first person narrator from whose point of view they will contribute to the new narrative.

This time, have groups work at their own speed to develop the story.

A mini storytelling festival might be held to feature the variety of tellings which the class will produce.

(d) Exploring inside stories

As we did with the *Lost Kingdom of Karnica*, some of the secrets (stories) inside the tale can be identified. (For example, How many attempts did Spider Woman require to send up a spinneret? what obstacles did she encounter? was the weather against her? and so on.)

Perhaps a chant could be invented for the making of the web.

Other stories might involve the circumstances under which the woman was whisked away to the Sky Pueblo or how the husband found Spider Woman.

(e) Exploring the outside stories

Finding the stories outside the story usually involves aspects of the story that are not central to it, but make interesting background. For example, Who is Spider Woman? why does she live apart? The class might make up a short story of her origin by creating three tableaux and linking them with voice-over narration. Making the story that the tribe painted about Spider Woman on the sides of their pueblos could take us into the realm of visual storytelling. I'm sure this could be the beginning of many episodes in the continuing story of Spider Woman.

Storytelling in the Community:

All the possibilities that exist for young people to collect stories in their own homes, neighborhoods and communities should not be overlooked. Capturing these tales on tape recorders then transcribing and illustrating them, help children to understand the role of stories in bridging the gap between child and adult across the generations. Such stories not only help children to define who they are, but help them gain a better understanding of their own family members. Family photographs are often one of the most effective ways these stories can be released.

We can encourage lots of informal storytelling with children. The range can extend from the most far-out fantasy to the stories about what has happened to us in our own lives. This can occur at specific times (storyhour) or as needed to relate past experience to present situations. This might include everything from a tale containing a variety of motifs to the eliptical stories we use to comment on anything and everything that is going on around us. (When the cat's away, the mice will play.)

Perhaps such activity will help children to truly grasp the meaning of I.B. Singer's reminder in *Naftali the Storyteller and His Horse, Sus* (Farrar, Straus & Giroux):

> *"When a day passes it is no longer there.*
> *What remains of it? Nothing more than a story.*
> *If stories weren't told or books weren't*
> *written, man would live like beasts — only*
> *for the day.*
> *Today, we live, but by tomorrow today*
> *will be a story.*
> *The whole world, all human life,*
> *is one long story."*

Appendix

Further reading and information on aspects of storytelling are provided in the following sources:

- Pellowski, Anne, *The World of Storytelling*, N.Y. R.R. Bowker and Co.
  A detailed history of storytelling throughout the world.
- Morgan, John and Rinvolucri, Mario, *Once Upon a Time: Using Stories in the Language Classroom*, London, Cambridge University Press.
  A practical resource book for teachers which includes activities on many aspects of oral language.
- Chambers, Aidan, *Introducing Books to Children*, London, Heinemann Educational.
  A practical exploration of ideas, methods and approaches for bringing children and books together. Contains a chapter on storytelling and reading aloud.
- Landsberg, Michele, *Michele Landsberg's Guide to Children's Books*, Penguin Canada Ltd.
  An excellent guide for parents and teachers who wish to help children find good books to read.
- Yolen, Jane, *Touch Magic*, N.Y. Philomel.
  The importance of passing on to children the great myths and folklore of the past is the subject of this lively and stimulating book.
- Benton, Michael and Fox, Geoff, *Teaching Literature Nine to Fourteen*
  An extremely useful book which emphasizes the interplay between reader and text and furnishes numerous practical applications for the teacher.
- Schafer, Murray R., *When Words Sing*, Toronto, Berandol.
  Dynamic activities which encourage children and adults to explore sound and the use of their own voices are provided by one of Canada's most exciting composers.
- Kaye, Cathryn Berger, *Word Works*, Boston, Little Brown and Company.
  This book, designed for children to use, invites readers to become actively involved as wordsmiths. The chapter on storytelling provides practical activities.
- Colwell, Eileen, *Storytelling*, London, The Bodley Head.
  Former children's librarian and noted storyteller Eileen Colwell shares her love and enthusiasm for storytelling in this practical guide for parents and teachers.
- Booth, David and Lundy, Charles, *Improvisation*, Learning Through Drama, Toronto, Academic Press.
  An insightful and practical student text, which features numerous approaches for working with young people and stories.

- Williamson, Duncan, *Fireside Tales of the Traveler Children*, N.Y. Harmony.

    Stories of an outcast minority group are featured in this fascinating book which contains a particularly interesting introduction noting the importance of storytelling to traveler children.

- Grimm, Jacob and Wilhelm, *Selected Tales*, Penguin.

    David Luke has translated most of the 65 tales in this important collection and has provided an extremely useful introduction to the work.

- Opie, Iona and Peter, *The Oxford Dictionary of Nursery Rhymes*, London, Oxford University Press.

    Included in this dictionary are more than 500 rhymes and songs as well as extensive information provided by the authors. (See also *The Oxford Nursery Rhyme Book* by the Opies.)

- Welty, Eudora, *One Writer's Beginnings*, Cambridge, Massachusetts, Harvard University Press.

    A major writer reveals how family and surroundings contributed to the shape of her writing.

National Association for the Preservation and Perpetuation of Storytelling (NAPPS), P.O. Box 309, Jonesborough, Tennessee 37659

Storytellers School of Toronto, 412-A College Street, Toronto, Ontario M5T 1T3.

Index

A

B

E

F

G

H

Acknowledgments

Every effort has been made to acknowledge all sources of material used in this book. The publishers would be grateful if any errors or omissions were pointed out, so that they may be corrected.

Acknowledgment is gratefully made for the use of the following copyright material:

Excerpt from "Advice From a Visiting Poet" from *Rainbow Writing* by Eve Merriam. Copyright © 1976 by Eve Merriam. Reprinted by permission of Marian Reiner for the author.

"The Bamboo Tower" by Jan Knappert in *Myths and Legends of the Congo*, by permission of the author.

"Crystal Rooster" from *Italian Folktales*, Selected and Retold by Italo Calvino, translated by George Martin, copyright © 1956 by Giulio Einaudi editore, s.p.a. English translation copyright © 1980 by Harcourt Brace Jovanovich, Inc. Reprinted by permission of Harcourt Brace Jovanovich, Inc.

"Day Peep" from *Ounce Dice Trice*, copyright Alastair Reid.

"I'm Tipingee, She's Tipingee, We're Tipingee, Too" from *The Magic Orange Tree And Other Haitian Folktales*, collected by Diane Wolkstein. Copyright © 1978 by Diane Wolkstein. Reprinted by permission of Alfred A. Knopf, Inc.

"JoJo" by Michael Rosen in *You Can't Catch Me*, by permission of Andre Deutsch, London.

King Nimrod's Tower by Leon Garfield and Michael Bragg. Copyright © 1982 by Leon Garfield. By permission of Lothrop, Lee & Shepard Books (A division of William Morrow & Company).

"The Loch Ness Monster's Song" by Edwin Morgan in *Poems of Thirty Years*, by permission of Carcanet Press Ltd., England.

"The Lost Kingdom of Karnica" by Richard Kennedy, by permission of the author.

"Mary Brown" from I. & P. Opie's *The Singing Game*, copyright Oxford University Press 1985.

"The Moonwuzo's Sea Song" by Cara Lockhart Smith in *Old Merlaine*, by permission of William Heinemann Ltd., London.

"My Father's Onion Sandwich" by Brian Doyle in *Up To Low*, by permission of Douglas & McIntyre Ltd., Vancouver.